C0-AAY-406

The Whale
Who
Wouldn't Die

The Whale
Who
Wouldn't Die

The True Story of "Miracle"

Paul Jeune

Follett Publishing Company
Chicago

Copyright © 1979 by Paul Jeune. All rights
reserved. No portion of this book may be used
or reproduced in any manner whatsoever
without written permission from the publisher
except in the case of brief quotations embodied
in critical reviews and articles. Manufactured in
the United States of America.

Library of Congress Cataloging in Publication Data

Jeune, Paul, 1951-
    The whale who wouldn't die.

    1. Killer whale—Legends and stories.
2. Wildlife rescue.   I. Title.
QL737.C432J48   639.97'953   79-2324
ISBN 0-695-81338-2

First Printing

FOR CHRISTINA
who is my best friend and my bride.
This book would have never been written
without her help and understanding.

ACKNOWLEDGEMENTS

No one will ever be completely sure about the first year of Miracle's life – the exact circumstances of her wounds or the depths of her pain and anguish. But probing detective work and months of analysis by whale experts led to several possible theories. It is the combination of these theories that forms the basis for the beginning of this story.

My appreciation in this regard is extended to Dr. Michael Bigg, of the Pacific Biological Station at Nanaimo, and Angus Matthews and Bob Wright of Sealand at Victoria. I must also thank Sealand's animal trainer, Cees Schrage, the husband and wife veterinary team of Jim and Judy McBain of Nanaimo, who, along with killer whale specialist Tag Gornall of Seattle, added medical support to the medical-rescue team during some of Miracle's crisis periods, and Sealand personnel as well as Oak Bay Marina office staff for interrupting busy schedules to add to my background knowledge of killer whales generally and Miracle's rescue specifically.

And a special thanks to Ken Hinkins for his unwavering support.

CHAPTER 1

A Whale is Born

A stranglehold of fog wept over everything it touched in the pre-dawn along Vancouver Island's east coast; and everything Bill Davis touched was wet, especially his aluminum skiff, which sweated clammily under the fog mist.

With the fog had settled a stillness. The only sounds were the muffled clanging of metal salmon fishing gear as Davis loaded it inside of the boat, a squeal of rubber rollers against the skiff bottom as it slipped from the trailer, and the wash of ceaseless wavelets as they spent themselves along the Menzies Bay shoreline.

It was mid-summer 1976. The sun was still an hour below British Columbia's Coast Range mountains. The fog wasn't unusual along the island's coast, but it wasn't usually as thick and would normally burn off with the rising sun. But this fog wouldn't burn off, it would take a strong wind to blow it through the channels and over the hills. There was no wind nor was there likely to be any.

Davis took his fishing seriously, although not fanatically, and he had apprenticed the craft of small boat handling well, so that the weather was no deterrent. The trip was one of his early morning, mid-week excursions – in the water by four, out by six-thirty, and to work at a nearby paper mill by eight. Sometimes he fished with a friend or his teenage son, but this day he enjoyed the thought of fishing alone.

Other than a full-brim, tan fishing hat, Davis was a patently forgettable man. At fifty years of age he was average height with a slim, unprepossessing build. Although not a shy person, he was unobtrusively quiet; his actions, when he loaded and cast off the boat, were not fast nor were they slow. As he motored the skiff away from the shoreline towards a small gut of water called Seymour Narrows, he pulled the hat further down on his head and bent the forward brim against the dampness. From shore his hunched figure in the stern dissolved into the dark and the mists, moments after his outboard engine sputtered to life.

Behind the fog curtain, and towards the west of Davis, Menzies Bay cut a deep, upside-down, dog's figure into the side of Vancouver Island. The dog's forelegs became Seymour Narrows – hemmed by Vancouver Island and Quadra Island which, with several other small islands, looked like stepping stones to the British Columbia mainland and the rest of Canada that stretched to the east. The Narrows bulged out to form Discovery Passage, Johnstone Strait, Broughton Strait, and Queen Charlotte Strait – all waters that cut the northern island from the mainland. To the southeast, the island coast scrawled its way towards the city of Victoria where the twenty-two-mile-wide Strait of Georgia moats the island from both mainland Canadian and United States territories.

Davis piloted the skiff almost halfway up the Narrows before throttling the two-cylinder outboard back to an idle. It didn't run smoothly at low speeds but squirmed and jiggled on its stern perch while he mounted a pair of fishing rods on opposite sides of the boat, made a last check of baited lures, and paid out line.

Although Davis's skiff was the only boat in the Narrows, he wasn't the only one fishing. Harbour seals that made homes along the rocky inshores of Menzies Bay were also waiting for the herring that would drift in with the rising tide. They gave little attention to the sputtering boat that nodded past them except to poke their heads a little further out of the water and scan it with each eye separately before arching a dive under water. Davis watched the roly-poly, torpedo shapes for several minutes as they squirmed just under the surface past the boat. There were more now than at first, maybe twenty; some chasing each other, some popping to the surface for a breath and quizzical look around, and still others bobbing along the surface like furry balloons.

Davis was changing tacks – zigzagging from the southern end of the Narrows to the northern end – when he got his first strike. The fisherman played his salmon for half an hour before landing it and had paid no attention to the occasional, daring seal that surfaced near the boat during the excitement. But when the lines were reset, and the skiff was headed back through the area where most of the seals were last seen, there was nothing. There were no telltale ripples in the water, just the quiet heaving of a ground swell.

The sun had risen over Davis's left shoulder, but hidden and diffused by the mists, it shed only a pallid grey light onto the greyer waters. He tried to look through the surface shimmer, but even in the soft light his reflection shielded the depths from squinting eyes so that he had to look through cupped hands. It was a long moment before he straightened. He had seen silver flashes of perch and herring as they flowed silently beneath the skiff. The flood tide had begun, but the disappearance of the seals bothered him.

The boat was again at the wide mouth of Menzies Bay and he turned to make a final tack to the centre of the Narrows before reeling in lines. When he neared Wilfred Point, before rounding it into the Narrows, he thought he heard the sound of heavy surf. But the fog played tricks, diffusing sound as it did light, so he dismissed it as the ground swell washing ashore on the rocky point. He cleared the rocks and was scarcely inside the channel when the sea, fifty feet to his starboard, parted and blew skyward in a loud rush of fish-tainted mist that was thicker and warmer than the fog. The noise startled Davis and he watched the black and white bulk of a killer whale gasp in another breath before dipping its head into a dive that left only the tiniest ripple. Davis took in the lines while another whale surfaced in the distance and spat out its breath with such force that it too could be heard over the spasmodic beat of the engine. Soon the entire channel seemed to pant with the explosive breaths. He began counting but tired of it when he reached fifty.

Curiosity kept Davis from retreating. The channel was now turbulent with the full force of the tide and the splashing whales – some would jump full length out of

the water and belly-flop into a dive. But caution kept him well out of their path. He huddled his skiff into the shallow nooks of the Narrows, throttling the engine just enough to keep the boat off the rocks as he watched.

He remained still a long while as the boat idled for shore, watching as the last whale was swallowed by a combination of water and mist. A duty to earn a living was the only thing that pulled Davis away.

He was unaware that at the same moment, less than five miles to the north, another event was taking place that would have a dramatic impact on his life. At the head of a secluded cove, in the warm shallows, a female killer whale swam in small circles. She was heavy and bulging with the final moments of pregnancy. Methodically she surfaced; blew the stale air from her lungs, sucked a new breath and vocalized, or squealed, before slipping below the surface again.

Less than a hundred feet seaward a large bull killer whale stretched his bulk almost three-quarters of the distance across the mouth of the bay. He lay quiet, partially submerged, with only the occasional movement of his powerful tail to keep him from drifting. His sensitive hearing was sharpened to detect anything that might threaten the birth.

The female arched through a slightly larger circle before surfacing in a cloud-spray of breath. She didn't dive again but continued the slow circling. Her breaths came shorter and shallower; her great girth sucked in and out and she quivered along her nineteen-foot length. She was in deep labour. When she stopped her circling, small tail fins began to protrude from the slit in the white expanse of her after-belly. The tail grew longer in moments, pulling behind it a smooth rubbery body. The bull, who had not moved until now, swam within ten feet of his mate. He watched as the baby's tail flukes began to whip gently from side to side and more of the small body slid into the water. The dorsal fin, which would eventually stand partially erect on the baby's back, was curved around the left side of the body. And an orange patch behind the fin gave the whale an identity as unmistakable as that of a human fingerprint. It too would change to resemble the white saddle patches of its parents, although the shape would remain unique.

The pectoral fins, the whale's steering gear, were folded snugly around the baby's chest; and finally the head slid from the mother. The bull dove quickly and had already placed one of his pectoral fins under the calf when the mother settled in on the other side. Together they raised the newborn to the surface for its first lungful of brackish air.

On the surface, the bull continued to lay close alongside the infant while the female swam circles around and below the new life. Finally, satisfied that all things were as they should be, she again positioned herself opposite the bull with the calf between them.

Throughout the day, and for several days to follow, the bull and female led the calf through a series of exercises that taught breathing, diving, the danger signal of tail slapping, and the whistles and squeals that make up their language. The bull left the bay for several hours each day, returning with fish and, if he was lucky, harbour seals which he would offer to his mate. The toothless calf, however, preferred its mother's warm, rich milk to the bull's shredded offerings.

But one morning the bull didn't go hunting. He swam restlessly back and forth outside the bay. The fog had blown away but the wind remained and tossed white frothing streamers of spray from wave to wave. In the sky, molten grey clouds scudded hurriedly out of the west. It was time to leave; to follow the salmon to the mouths of the rivers before the fish made their final trek upstream to lay and fertilize eggs and die. The female nudged the calf, vocalizing at the same time. Together they swam to the bull, now waiting in mid-bay; the calf slid between the parents and the trio swam into the channels.

Davis never again saw pods of killer whales in the same numbers he did on that foggy summer morning. Nor did he think much about them. And it is reasonable to say the whales gave little thought to any of the fishermen they passed as they continued their southward quest for food.

CHAPTER 2

The Depths of Sadness

A crisp warning of autumn filled the air when the baby whale and its parents joined the group at the gaping mouth of the Fraser River, which spews into the sea along the southern mainland coast near the Canadian-United States border. There were only half as many in the pack as there had been when Davis saw them; several leaders had taken their pods to the mouths of other rivers and streams that finger seaward from the mountainous interior of the mainland north of the Fraser.

The Fraser has always been a muddy, ravaging river, taunting man, animal, and fish for centuries. Into the northeast, towards its minute beginnings, it spawns from hundreds of tributaries and flows from scores of obscure

17

lakes. It gains full strength only a few miles from the ocean after being joined by its largest tributary, the Thompson River. And the full fury of that strength is squeezed between a narrow rock gorge called Hell's Gate – a thrashing, watery oblivion so named because of the threat it posed to early explorers. It used to meet the sea at a much earlier point but countless ages of erosion upstream have built a vast delta now used as farmland. When the river does reach the ocean it is almost tame and drops silt in an ever-widening arc near the mouth. It is in these soft shallows that the killer whales wait for the salmon.

It was a strange experience for the baby whale – the youngest from a family pod of ten. The mixture of salt and fresh water was curious and so was the lack of buoyancy. The calf was forever trying to spit the irritating silt from its mouth, using its powerful tongue as a piston to drive the water out in long streams. But the silt was always there, as was the pungent taste of industrial waste that spilt continuously from huddles of factories along the river's banks.

Nothing was to deter the hunters–slight discomforts were a small price for a feast of salmon. The days were spent chasing cod and other bottom fish outside the shallows, and chasing early salmon part way up the river. There were also play times; hours of high-speed chases and full-length jumps that would momentarily halt the work force in the nearby metropolis of Vancouver as secretaries and executives rose from meetings and harried schedules to watch the sight from glass-fronted highrise buildings.

More than once, daydreaming harbour tug crews and wearied fishermen, laying a course for home, were jolted to their senses by the more mischievous whales which would spring full length from the water beside the boats and peer sombre-faced into the wheel-houses – more often than not to meet the wide-eyed gaze of the skipper. It is said, although not with proper verification, that the whales did more in a single jump for one hard-bitten skipper than Alcoholics Anonymous could have done in twenty-five years.

The fun and games were limited for two of the whales, though; their calf demanded much of their time. Be-tween feedings – and the calf nursed dozens of times each day – the parents were continually leading and pushing the baby away from endless lines of boats that ran the gamut from small outboard-powered skiffs and deep-keeled sailboats to ocean-splitting freighters. Un-derwater the drone and whine of engines never stop-ped, although it subsided slightly at night.

The calf's age could be measured in weeks but al-ready signs of maturing were evident. Its dorsal fin stood partially erect and the orange saddle patch was mellow-ing, showing blotches of adult white. The calf had not increased its eight-foot birth size by more than a few inches but had filled out with layers of protective fat. Continual practising of shallow dives had strengthened the side-protruding pectoral fins so that they were be-coming useful limbs instead of flopping encumbrances. The first of forty or more conically shaped teeth were poking through the wide expanse of gums and, like all teething animals, the calf had an overwhelming urge to bite.

When it began biting at its mother's fins she decided on a solid supplement to the calf's milk diet. Several times a day she would catch a small salmon and fillet it by snapping it through the water while hanging onto the head. Although killer whales don't chew their food as such, the calf would play with the fillets and bite them unmercifully before swallowing.

It was less than a week after the whales arrived when thousands of salmon streamed to the mouth of the river to start their inland journey. The whales feasted for more than a month before disappearing silently when the run fell off to little more than a trickle. The pods split up and the calf and its group made their way across the Strait of Georgia to a scatter of islands, reefs, and channels off southeastern Vancouver Island, called the Gulf Islands. The waters were warm and sheltered and many winter salmon – those not mature enough to make the trip upstream – swam near the reefs. It was a good and safe place for the young whale to grow; a rich place for the nursing mother to feed.

Unlike man, killer whales do not dwell in one small area. They are not migratory in the true sense, but a never-ending search for food makes them nomadic. The pod moved naturally and tirelessly from island shoal to island shoal, through a maze of channels that ran through underwater valleys and over small submarine mountains.

The fiery leaves of late autumn had turned brown and all but the staunchest had fallen. The fog and rain of an almost forgotten miserable summer had disappeared and, though the storms of November had driven in hard, crisp sunny days moved in back to back for half a month. Along the shore, in sheltered coves, rows of commercial fishing boats were moored to the long arms of docks. On the water sports fishermen crowded the shoals to hook one of the remaining salmon.

For the most part the whales moved unseen, past the docks, around the fishermen and along the shoreline, hunting any food that came within range of their sonar bounces.

20

During the preceding months the whales had been able to find more salmon than they could eat. But, as salmon are prone to do, they disappeared from the islands suddenly and the pod was forced to exist mostly on stored fat. The larger whales could theoretically live for months on the internal stores but food was crucial for the mother whale – she needed constant nourishment to feed her suckling calf. Yet the mother never had any fear that her needs, and the needs of the baby whale, would not be met. Her ancestors, until the beginning of their time in the sea, had lived under a social order that demanded responsibility to each other. She knew the pod would hunt food for her, and even sacrifice their lives if the need arose.

Killer whales, despite the fact that they are the most feared predator in the oceans in the absence of the most voracious of sharks, are not naturally blood thirsty. They kill only to eat and will feed on whatever is most plentiful and easiest to hunt. When the salmon left the Gulf Islands the whales turned to the numerous sea lions in an effort to feed the mother whale. There was only one fast rule during these hunts; the calf and its mother stayed hidden if and when the pod moved in to bring down one of the animals. It was a security measure. An enraged, maimed sea lion, weighing anywhere from 1,000 to 2,000 pounds, would attack anything in its path – a slow-moving mother and calf would be prime targets for the furious animal.

There was no hunting skill involved when a hapless young stellar sea lion swam around a rocky point into the path of the hunters. But good fortune had its limits.

Blocked from view on the other side of the point a boy not yet out of his teens struggled with his boat, a wallowing hulk of a commercial gillnet boat – this his initiation into a fisherman's manhood. It was more of a home to

21

the worm-like teredos that lived in her planks than an investment to the unlucky lad who had just bought her. She had laid dock-bound and neglected for half a decade, her original skipper and builder dead of old age. The boy had bartered with the widow – though it wasn't much of a barter; he was the first to show interest in the boat since it had been laid up. Two years of deck-hand's wages went into rebuilding the rusting engine, with scarcely enough left to buy gillnet.

As the whales began to chase down the sea lion, the boy was piloting the boat back to the mooring docks from a raft-dock in a nearby bay where he had wound the net on his drum. The boat looked almost seaworthy as it snored through the channel, but ancient gear, anchored with corroding bolts, was straining throughout the craft. Without warning a dog catch, holding the drum from spinning, shattered, and a half-mile of net began tumbling overboard. The entire net was in the water – the trailing end tethered to the drum by a short nylon line – by the time the engine was stopped and the cursing boy was on the stern deck.

The long strands of net and wire reinforcement carried the noise of the squealing drum into the depths. The sounds momentarily stopped the sea lion and the whales made a final bloody dash. Although the fight was short-lived, the first taste of current carried blood, and the squealing net drum scared the calf. In blind fright it thrashed out of its hiding cove into the channel on the opposite side of the point. The mother swam and squealed after the youngster, but before the calf could turn, it became ensnared in the drifting net. The alarm was sounded; eight whales dropped their prey, surfaced to gulp fresh air, and drove towards the calf. Row after row of fist-sized teeth hammered through the strands and the water boiled chaotically.

The boy cursed as his dreams were splayed like a spider web. He ran to the wheelhouse and shouldered a rifle. He didn't aim but fired fast as the whales surfaced to breathe.

The tide spread whale blood in molten patterns behind the boat just as it had carried the net. Crimson spume washed over the deck as wounded whales surfaced and blew a second time, only to be met again by rifle fire. Angrily the boy emptied a dozen boxes of lead into the whales until there was only one shot left. A series of four fins broke the water to the starboard but they were out of range and swimming away.

Under water the fight had been paid for heavily. The calf was still suspended in the net, caught at this point by only its tail flukes. The rest of the bondage had been ripped and shredded by the adults. On the channel bottom, five carcasses oozed bloody streams, and air bubbles chortled to the surface. Two of the dead were the young whale's parents. The surviving adults fled under fire only because they believed the calf already dead – and it nearly was. The young whale would have drowned had the boy not cut the anchor rope to keep the now useless net from getting tangled in the propeller. As it fell loose the calf was able to wrench free. With barely enough energy to surface, the whale spouted just twenty feet behind the boat.

On deck the boy aimed the rifle one last time.

The bullet cut through the black flesh behind the dorsal fin, crashed into a bone and split, blasting two gaping exit wounds in the calf's side. The force hurled the whale onto its side and it curled convulsively in pain. The wound, coupled with exhaustion from the fight, left the calf temporarily paralyzed. It lay stunned and in shock for more than a minute, and the boy would have killed it if he'd had another shot. Then it sucked its first breath since surfacing and cried a long, soft squeal. After another breath it slowly arched under water.

Although unheard on the surface, the squeals continued under water the remainder of the day, into the night, and for many days and nights to come, as the wounded calf searched for the pod survivors. Travelling on hope it turned south, weaving a drunken path through the Gulf Islands. Several days later, after the first surge of panic and shock had diminished, the calf slithered along the muddy bottom of a still bay, rubbing clay into its wounds to stop the bleeding. The once smooth skin was rippled and cracked with abrasions from the net, and long, wide scratches circled its back where the other whales had bitten at the strands.

The weeks passed and agonized into a month. The orphan hungered, not only for the food it couldn't catch, but for the security of a family. The calf knew the pod – or what was left of it – would at least try to satisfy both needs if it could be found. But the search was almost impossible. The young whale had not been alive long enough to know much about the pod's submarine highways or their unmarked destinations.

*   *   *

The chill of the first and only snowfall that winter, in mid-January laid an ice-cream covering over the Gulf Islands, but the calf gave little notice or thought to it. It had fed a little on the stinking carcass of a harbour seal that had floated to the surface from a watery grave. Although the rotting flesh gave the baby whale stomach cramps for nearly a week, it also gave it new strength and hope.

For the rest of the winter, until mid-March, the whale

continued its never-ending search for the pod and easy food. The search was never methodical and the baby's blind panic drove it in loops and circles through the Gulf Island channels. At one point, its cries for help were answered and it swam frantically to a pod of whales travelling lazily through one of the larger channels. It wasn't the calf's pod but they were the first whales the baby had seen since being orphaned. It swam south with them for two days, crossing the unseen border into United States waters. But killer whales, though strongly social animals, have a code that prevents them from adopting strays, and on the third day the baby swam away from the pod, back to the channels it had left so hopefully.

The calf probably would have been content to wait in the Gulf Islands – and probably would have died there – had two young boys in a small outboard-powered dinghy not spotted it. The calf was now spending most of its time floating near the surface, with just a portion of its white saddle patch and dorsal fin showing.

At first the boys thought the small whale was sleeping or dead. They began circling it, closing in a little more with each turn, until finally the whale spouted a shallow stream of breath-mist. The blast scared the boys and they backed the boat several yards away. But bravery among small boys comes in pairs and results from double dares. The boy in the bow dared the other to take the boat closer and the boy steering bet the other he couldn't touch the whale with a paddle. The calf might have stayed quiet had the boy who was steering not lost control of the dinghy at a crucial moment, and run the bow up on the whale's back. As the baby sounded and the boat leaped forward again, the propeller dug deep gouges just behind the whale's blow hole.

The calf was wracked with pain. The bullet wounds were becoming increasingly infected with each passing day, hunger was a constant, gnawing torture and now, with each breath, it gulped blood running from the propeller gashes. But worst of all was the hurt of loneliness.

It was several weeks before the propeller wounds closed enough to stop bleeding completely, but not before infection set in. Medically the young whale should have died months earlier – the lack of food alone would have taken life from most killer whales the same age. But there was something in the calf, deeper and stronger than the wounds and more constant than the hunger, that kept the struggle alive.

Summoning each ounce of its will power, the young whale followed an instinct; a hunch that better times lay to the north. Although adult whales usually cruise at ten miles an hour, it was a struggle for the calf to reach a quarter of that speed, and then only for short distances. It was three and a half months before it got to the north end of the Gulf Islands, slightly more than a hundred miles from its starting point at the southern end of the island chain.

The whale could have made the journey in less than a month, even in its tenuous condition, but hunger and pain had jammed its inbuilt sonar system and often it would spend the better part of a day stranded on a sand bar. In those situations the tide and currents were allies, working to help the calf free itself. But more often the early spring tides, bottlenecking in the narrow island channels, overpowered the weakening whale and pushed it backwards. Towards the northern end of the islands the calf learned to stop fighting the currents and swam only when the tides surged north.

It is at the northern tip of the archipelago where Nanaimo Harbour cuts a grimy chunk from Vancouver Island and, against what would be the better instincts of most killer whales, where the young whale sought refuge. Possibly the never-ending drone of freighters, fishing boats, and pleasure craft reminded the baby of happier moments at the mouth of the Fraser River. Whatever the reason, it swam into the deepest recesses of the potent bay, drawing close to the noise and confusion of a lumber loading dock. In these muddy waters the calf ceased to be alone, although it probably never realized it.

*   *   *

At the other end of the bay, in a sprawl of seaside offices, a group of men earned their living by researching and counting killer whales. They were marine biologists and the collage of buildings housed the Federal Fisheries Pacific Biological Station.

The killer whale research team, headed by Dr. Michael Bigg, a young, extremely dedicated and energetic man, had developed a whale reporting system that fanned over the island. Bigg had gathered, and learned to rely on, a string of volunteers who reported whale sightings and movements to the researchers. Since 1971, when the project was initiated, unofficial volunteers – anyone who could dial a telephone – had often been over-enthusiastic about making their reports. It was from one of these sources that Bigg heard the dubious report about the young calf. He recalled the incident, saying: "We got a call July fourth that a whale was swimming among the log booms. I couldn't believe it and asked the caller to tell me about the seal he'd really seen, but he was adamant it was a small whale."

Unwilling to log the sighting until it had been proven, Bigg pushed aside a dozen reports of bona fide sightings he had been working on, and drove to the other side of the bay. Actually finding a whale in the murky water was a shock to the scientist – it contravened every piece of data and shred of evidence the team had been able to collect on the animals. Never before had a young killer whale – and rarely an adult – been sighted on its own.

"Unlike any other whales, killer whales have a very strong family unit and as far as we know that family lasts forever, being replenished by young as over-mature animals die off," Bigg said later. "We knew something strange had happened and was happening in the case of this whale."

After taking pictures of the calf's dorsal fin and saddle patch to add to the team's whale identification file, Bigg returned to the office. The sighting continued to bother him and his anxiety appeared in a log report: "Contact with a single baby whale is extremely unusual, it has never before been recorded. The animal's actions were not normal, it was swimming erratically back and forth and seemed highly agitated."

To fully grasp the impact of the report is to understand the ideals of the scientist. Very little is ever unusual – let alone extremely unusual – until it can be proven so. Few theories are ever based on gut feelings. When the whale was sighted, Bigg's team had completed slightly more than six years' research. New information was changing their concept of the killer whale daily – they were still learning what was normal – yet Bigg was convinced the calf was not normal. In concluding the report, Bigg noted that time was probably the young whale's strongest ally; that, in time, the calf would probably locate its pod and lead a normal life. He had no way of knowing that time was running out for the baby whale or that he, Bigg, would be a major influence in the calf's life.

Bigg had no sooner completed the reports and received the first prints of the fin and saddle patch photographs, when a telephone call informed him that the calf had disappeared. Later the same day a caller reported spotting a lone whale near Protection Island off Nanaimo Harbour.

Using the last of its strength, the calf had continued the northward search for its pod. It had stayed in Nanaimo Harbour only half a day, long enough to realize the search couldn't end in those dirty waters.

For two weeks, the journey was tracked by phone calls reporting the oddity of a lone baby whale. On a large cork-backed chart, stuck to the cement wall of a basement office, Bigg traced the calf's progress with colour-headed pins which marked the areas of sightings. The last pin punctured the chart about one hundred and twenty-five miles north of Nanaimo, just south of the fishing-lumbering town of Campbell River.

The calf had managed to swim another several miles further north into the sparsely populated area of Menzies Bay. Depleted of strength and quickly losing the will to fight, the orphan crept into the bay shortly after nightfall. It edged along a sandbar, ironically named Defender Shoal, and swam into the inner bay through a broad channel at the northern end. Wanting only to rest its pain-stiffened body, the whale glided into the isolated shallows in the far northern corner and lay in the soft sand less than a fathom below the surface. It broke the top of the water only to breathe.

Though the calf, now almost a year old, had given up the struggle for survival, as well as the frantic search for its pod, death did not come fast. Life trickled out slowly and the pain stretched unmercifully into days and weeks.

CHAPTER 3

An End — A Beginning

On Tuesday, August 2, 1977, the early-morning sun burned off a light fog over Menzies Bay and promised to further bake the already dry, brown countryside.

It was the middle of a heat wave. For more than two weeks the mercury in Fahrenheit thermometers had been driven past the ninety mark. Even an hour after dawn, at 6:00, the sun's rays were so intense that anyone within the reach of them could wear nothing but the lightest of clothes. By 7:30, in cities and towns up and down the coast, the first lines of work-bound traffic snarled into place. An hour later, employees – and many employers – without the benefit of air conditioning, began shedding neckties to gain what comfort they could from open collars. The few who worked within the cool currents of air conditioning spent the day dreading the drive home and the heat of their non-air conditioned houses.

But the heat was news in a climate where a midsummer temperature of seventy-five to eighty degrees is considered more than adequate. By noon, two editors of small weekly newspapers within fifty miles of Menzies Bay had unknowingly hit upon the same idea. Both editors had sent a photographer and a reporter into the town centres to fry eggs on the sidewalks to graphically illustrate the intensity of the heat.

Bill Davis was up before dawn that day. He ate a bacon-and-eggs breakfast and checked a booklet of tide tables before leaving for work. He was one of the lucky ones – the area of the mill in which he worked was air conditioned, and the sun fell off his house about 3:00 in the afternoon, so that it cooled off slightly by the time he arrived back home. The evening before he had polished his best fishing lures and readied and stowed his rods. A neighbour, and long-time fishing partner, Gerry Kool, had agreed to try fishing with him after work.

On the way to Menzies Bay the two fishermen stopped at the Campbell River fishermen's wharf, clambered onto a barge, moored near the shore-end of the pier, and bought a bucket of live herring for bait. But, by the time they had made the eight-mile drive to the boat launching ramp, the fish had died from the heat and were floating at the top of the sloshing bucket of water. Davis and Kool had little time to agonize over their wasted investment before a bronze-tanned girl in her early teens approached them. She seemed to be stopping to talk to all the fishermen – those coming back from fishing and the ones just starting out.

"It's lousy fishing," she said through Davis's open truck window.

"How so?" asked Davis.

"Only fish in is barely legal," she said. "Everyone that's back says the fish aren't biting because of the killer whale along the inside of the bay."

"Never heard of a killer whale being on the inside before. Is it still there?"

"I think so. The last group of guys said they saw it about half an hour ago."

"Well, since we're here we might as well try fishing. Can't do worse than most of the others," Davis said, as much to Kool as to the girl.

"Sure. Just thought I'd tell you what to expect," she said, already heading for the next fisherman at the ramp.

Davis learned later that the first person to see the whale was a rather blanched looking scuba diver. Hunting for crabs under rock beds that peppered the bottom of the inside bay, the diver had swum into the little-used northern corner and had inadvertently come nose to nose with the whale. Curiosity wasn't one of his stronger virtues, and witnesses are still willing to wager a bet that the diver could have outswum an Olympic gold medalist in his hurry to reach shore.

Kool knew enough not to ask any questions when Davis headed the aluminum skiff towards the inside bay instead of along the outside harbour where everyone else was fishing. In fact, he knew before the boat left the trailer that his fishing partner would want to take at least one quick look at the whale. Davis had always held a certain curiosity about his surroundings and there was no reason why this time around should be any different.

When he neared the north end of the shoal that divided the inside and outside bays, Davis cut a sharp turn to port, expertly missing the shallows. Once inside the bay he throttled the engine back to a sputtering idle and angled the boat southward. Nothing moved on the inside except the boat. Although still burning hot, the sun was starting to slip towards the dry hills of the Vancouver Island interior. In its descent it shot rays through a gaping valley directly into the northern corner of Menzies Bay, in what seemed a final effort to make the waters boil.

The heat prickled the skin of the two men but they sat motionless, turning only their heads in sweeping gazes. After several minutes, when it seemed the heat and glare would force the men to leave, they heard a faint noise above the beat of the engine. Davis stopped the outboard and the men stared out of the boat in opposite directions in an effort to find the source of the sound. At first Davis couldn't be sure of what he saw – even through sunglasses the glare was making his eyes water and blurring his vision – but he thought it was a small whale fin about two hundred yards in front of the boat. Just as Davis was about to say something, Kool pointed at the same object.

Davis restarted the engine and the boat cruised slowly down on the animal. The whale didn't move until the boat was within a hundred feet and then it disappeared under water. Even at that distance the whale didn't look right to Davis. The normally black skin appeared to have large patches of brown slime on it. Again Davis shut the engine off and the two men sat waiting quietly.

In less than five minutes the baby whale surfaced again. This time the boat got within fifty feet. It was close enough for both men to see strange white tips on the otherwise black dorsal fin that stood off the whale's back. While Davis and Kool scanned the waters in an effort to locate the baby's pod, the whale swam away from the boat and submerged.

"It didn't look right. Not at all," Davis remembered. "I didn't know much about killer whales, and still don't for that matter, but I could tell she wasn't swimming well. She was sluggish, kind of clumsy, not graceful like all the other killer whales I'd seen. When she submerged it wasn't a dive – she just sort of sank. The same when she came up for air, she didn't break the surface like they mostly do, just slowly appeared."

The next time the whale surfaced, both men got the same idea simultaneously. And they both laughed as they caught each other eyeing the bucket of freshly dead herring. It was agreed that Davis should be the first to try feeding the whale. The men again managed to put the boat within fifty feet of the animal and just as it began to submerge, Davis heaved a herring that landed within several feet of the whale's nose. The baby clumsily aborted the dive and swallowed the fish.

Kool threw the next herring, but purposely delivered it about three feet closer to the boat than the first fish. The men took turns throwing, each fish landing slightly closer to the boat than the preceding one, until the whale was within twenty feet of the skiff. It was then that the men could see the scars of the propeller wounds behind the blow hole – although neither one could have guessed what tragedies lay behind the gouges or just how sick the animal was.

Davis threw out several more herring but the baby wouldn't come any closer. After the last fish had been thrown, the men talked quietly and watched the whale float near the surface. Finally realizing there were no more fish, the baby sounded.

Despite the loss of their bait, Kool and Davis decided to motor into the outer bay and try the evening fishing. Both men re-rigged their rods with artificial lures before strapping them into holders on either side of the skiff. It was a half-hearted gesture at best – the exercise of setting out the line – and was probably why they returned empty-handed. Neither of the men concentrated much on fishing that evening. Both of them had retreated into their own thoughts about the whale while the boat sputtered back and forth across the bay.

Each day brought the orphaned whale closer to death. Although the bottom of the bay was rich in crabs and bottom fish, the baby had no knowledge of how to catch them. And even if it had developed the expertise of a hunter, it lacked the strength required for a chase. The handful of herring that Davis and Kool had thrown was the first food the whale had eaten in more than two months. The propeller gashes and bullet wounds had healed superficially but the weakened condition of the animal allowed infection to run rampant. Worm-like parasites, ingested through the chunks of rotting meat the whale had eaten on several occasions, were boring holes through the black exterior of the baby as they squirmed their way to the outside.

The brown, slimy patches covering large portions of the animal were actually an algae growth. The heat wave had pushed the water temperature in the inside bay to more than sixty degrees and had allowed the algae to grow prolifically; the almost motionless bulk of the killer whale gave it a fine home. The white tips on the fins were the start of a skin-rotting fungus.

The orphan had been in the bay for little more than two weeks, waiting patiently and painfully for death to erase the suffering. Although the unusual stretch of high temperatures had forced hundreds of people to the seashore, the whale remained undetected until the chance meeting with the diver. Wanting nothing more

to do with humans since the initial conflict, the baby wisely kept to the north end of the bay where passersby mistook it for one of the resident harbour seals.

Davis made no attempt to see the whale again that night. Dusk was fast closing into darkness when the two men returned to the ramp and Davis feared any move to spot the baby in the dark might run afoul and cause injury to the animal. Despite his best efforts he was unable to sleep much when he got to bed. And when he did sleep it was in the company of fitful dreams about the lone baby. He was probably crazy, he thought as he boiled water for coffee during the early morning hours.

Davis's wife, Lois, wasn't surprised to find her husband's side of the bed empty when she woke to sounds in the kitchen at 4:00 A.M. She had long been used to his early risings in preparation of fishing trips, but his forfeiture of the bed that morning was a blessing. She could now get some uninterrupted sleep, she thought, as she rolled into the centre of the bed.

Davis gulped down six mugs of coffee and chain smoked through the hour before dawn. He heard, but did not listen to, the nocturnal noises of the house – the creaking and groaning of the wood, the clicking noises of birds walking along the eaves outside and the intermittent hum of the refrigerator. He tried to reason himself out of the growing affection he felt for, and baseless worry he had about, the whale. He knew nothing about killer whales, he told himself. Just because the young whale had ventured into waters never before inhabited by killer whales didn't mean things weren't normal. Surely a whale travelling by itself isn't cause for alarm. The brown patches and white blotches were probably quite normal – something that happens to whales this time of the year. The animal was probably slow moving because of the heat.

As valiantly as reasoning fought in the internal struggle, there was never much of a contest. By the time the Wednesday morning sun had poked its first shafts of light between the branches of the fir tree outside Davis's Campbell River home, he was closing the kitchen door quietly behind him. This time there were no fishing rods tucked behind the seat of the four-wheel-drive truck, just the boat trailer bouncing obediently in the wake of the fast-moving vehicle. Davis made his first stop at Fishermen's Wharf to buy herring, as he had done the evening before. But this time he felt guilty about his purchase.

The owner of the barge and seller of the herring was Alex Hunt, a slimly built but tough-as-nails commercial fisherman who worked long gruelling hours, not only to catch the fish, but to sell them as well. Since most fishermen – especially commercial seine-boat men – don't even feign any affection for killer whales, Davis did the natural thing when placing his order. He lied.

"Need some bait for cut-plugs," he called over the counter to Hunt. "About three dozen if you've got them. And the bigger you can get them, the better."

There. He'd got it out – sounded convincing too. But he still felt guilty. He'd been good friends with Hunt almost since the day he'd moved to Campbell River twenty years ago. It wasn't easy to lie to a friend.

The drive to the bay seemed like it would never end. As Davis ploughed off the main highway onto the half-mile-long gravel road to the boat ramp, he reluctantly closed the truck windows. The desert-dry dust encompassed the truck in grey billows and covered the boat and trailer with a fine, dirty powder.

Davis felt half foolish and half expectant as he guided the boat around the shoal into the inner bay. In one way he hoped the whale had disappeared – but in another way he hoped desperately against that wish. Once in the bay he didn't have much time to think about it. The whale surfaced almost immediately in a shallow mist of breath, halfway across the three-hundred-foot width of the northern end of the bay and directly in front of the boat. Davis stopped the engine with one hand and threw a herring with the other. The fish landed halfway between the whale and the skiff. The baby sounded, swam the twenty-five feet under water, and grabbed the sinking herring before it reached the bottom. When the whale surfaced, Davis threw another fish, this time closer to the boat. He kept repeating the exercise until the whale was within two feet of the skiff.

Davis had long been in the habit of keeping a camera with his fishing kit. The night before he had taken some distant shots of the whale but nothing compared to the close-up pictures he was now able to get. Between tosses of herring he quickly focussed the camera, trying to catch the whale in as many different poses as possible. At one point, he took too long between fish and the baby sounded. It was then that he learned that his affection was being returned by this strange whale.

He started the engine to look for the calf, only to find it had popped to the surface beside the boat before it was under way. He let the baby sound again and then restarted the engine; he repeated it a third time. Each time the whale would surface beside the boat. It was apparent the whale identified Davis by the sound of his engine. He fed the remaining herring to the baby in fast succession, keeping one last one in the boat. After several more pictures, he threw out the last fish, started the engine, and sped for the launching ramp, hoping the whale wouldn't follow him out of the bay.

The drive home was fast – almost too fast – and it was filled with plans, as opposed to the doubts that had plagued him on the way to the bay. When he arrived home, Lois was eating breakfast. The coffee she gave her husband went untouched as he told her of his latest encounter with the whale. And he told her of a dozen ideas – not least of which was a camping trip to Menzies Bay starting that night. Although somewhat puzzled about the need for a mid-week camping expedition, she agreed.

Kool – who also owned a truck and camper – was on a five-day weekend from his job at the mill and quickly agreed to go when Davis made the proposal.

After returning home from work that afternoon, Davis packed the camper, met Kool and his wife, and drove to Menzies Bay.

Davis and Kool had no sooner made camp and finished a hastily prepared supper before they were guiding the little skiff into the shallows of the inside bay. It had been cool under the alder trees where the campers were parked beside the boat ramp. But in the middle of the bay the 7:00 sun was still hot, wrapping the men in a breezeless water-reflected heat.

This time there was no waiting. The baby whale surfaced beside the boat even before it had stopped. Then it spotted Kool in the bow and sounded again, surfacing fifty feet away. It was half an hour before the men lured the whale to the side of the boat again. Davis then tried something daring – feeding the whale out of his hand.

"I think I was more nervous than the whale was,"

Davis recalled. "I'd wait until she was just about to take the fish, then I would drop it towards her and she would grab it. We were both nervous – it was a touchy proposition. She's got a big mouth, not to mention the teeth. Eventually both of us got braver and she would gently take the fish directly from my hand. I tried to touch her at that point but her body would flex away as soon as I moved my free hand towards her – you could see her watching with one eye all the time."

Davis's association with the whale had been very much a secret, although news of it was spreading rapidly among family members and close friends. But word of the events started to leak out shortly after dark that night.

Both men stayed awake well after sunset, talking and pacing the few feet to the edge of the beach, straining to catch a glimpse of the whale even though it would have been impossible to see it in the far reaches of the bay in the dark.

They thought all the evening fishermen had returned home; that was until they heard the high-pitched whine of a powerful outboard and saw it speedily pushing a small boat to shore. The engine stopped just off the boat ramp and the boat glided in the remainder of the distance. It was a couple of men whom Davis worked with. The four men talked fishing for a while until one of the newcomers said he'd seen Davis with the whale. Reluctantly Davis told his story. Surprisingly the men were sympathetic and promised to bring enough herring on their next trip to help feed the animal.

Davis slept better that night just knowing he was closer to the whale.

Thursday broke into daylight in the same threatening way it had done for two and a half weeks. It was going to be another scorcher. A haze that had filled in the valleys during the night and formed long, smoke-like tendrils along the shoreline, evaporated within minutes of sunrise. Even people who enjoyed the warmth of summer looked skyward in hope of seeing clouds. For most people, the clear sky meant another day of heat exhaustion – another day when simple tasks became sweat-laden chores. For Davis it meant the whale would have to suffer through another day of increasing water temperatures. He fed the calf quickly before driving to work.

At the mill the usual talk of fishing was replaced by rumours of "Davis's whale," and he spent a large part of the day answering questions and retelling his story. During the day, Kool, his wife and Davis's wife stood a distant sentry over the whale, repeatedly scanning the bay with binoculars. They were especially watchful of boats entering the inner bay, fearful the whale would surface unwittingly at the sound of any engine and be cut by propellers.

After work Davis made his usual stop for herring, on the way to camp. A number of fishermen from the mill had been there earlier, and had told Hunt about Davis and the whale, while fulfilling a promise to buy herring for the animal. By the time he left the bait barge, Davis wasn't quite sure what had happened – he still wasn't sure when he reached the bay; Hunt had refused all payment for the herring and he would continue to donate fish for the remainder of the whale's days in Menzies Bay.

When Davis reached the campers he found a group of friends and relatives, eager to see the whale. They had all brought buckets of herring to cover the cost of admission. Many of the people, including Davis, had raided their own stores of frozen bait.

After his own hurried supper, Davis marshalled a small squadron of dinghys to the entrance of the inner bay and left them and their occupants to wait at the edge of the shoal. The calf either didn't notice, or chose to ignore, the spectators and surfaced beside Davis's boat as soon as it entered the bay. He dropped a fresh herring in the calf's mouth and then threw it a frozen fish.

"She wasn't fussy about the first frozen herring," Davis later said. "I guess she didn't know what it was – just kind of played with it a long while before swallowing it."

After that, Davis alternated frozen and fresh fish to the satisfaction of the baby whale. That particular feeding was probably the most profound moment in the relationship between the whale and the man. It was the first time Davis was able to touch the baby and it led the way to what he later called "touch communication." Gently Davis moved his hands over the back of the calf and found what the algae had been able to conceal – the curved rows of teeth marks left by the baby's pod when they had tried to free it from the net. But it was only when he found what, even then, he correctly identified as bullet wounds, that he began to realize the misery the calf was suffering. He only barely kept from being physically ill when the baby quivered as his touch neared the wound. The mystery of the lone calf and its needs then started to become clearly defined to Davis.

"I believe she was trying to make friends with anybody – trying to orient herself with some other body or animal, or anything. There are a lot of seals in the bay. They possibly attracted her. Possibly she thought she could find companionship with them," Davis said.

Although he wasn't sure, Davis was beginning to

suspect his meagre offerings of fish were forming the bulk of the whale's food. Yet this was only one of several mounting problems confronting both the man and the animal.

By Friday night it seemed as though half of Campbell River had heard of the whale, though the news media still hadn't got wind of it. People began gathering at the edge of the shore, and that in itself didn't bother Davis. It was the armada of power boats filing in and out of the bay that concerned him most – and the fact that the whale was becoming drawn to boat motors. Most of his time that night was spent waving down boatloads of curiosity seekers and asking them to slow down so they wouldn't run over the calf.

If Davis was living in a nightmare of concern, the whale was oblivious and seemed to be enjoying the attention. It started making rounds between the incoming boats, mooching what it could before swimming on to the next. The calf was still painfully slow moving, though, and easily frightened. It would submerge for two or three minutes at the sound of a fast-moving boat, even when it was eating.

Any fears that Davis might have had about loyalty on the part of the whale were banished as soon as he started his outboard engine. The motor would run less than thirty seconds before the calf was either at Davis's side or moving in his direction. If he put the engine in gear the baby would follow ten feet behind the boat regardless of who else was in the bay.

Friday was just a forerunner of what the weekend was to bring. Saturday and Sunday melted into one chaotic haze for both Davis and Kool. More than thirty boats crammed into the bay both days, forcing the two men to stay with the whale constantly. And while the boats continued to speed into the bay, the men continued to wave them down, asking, warning, and pleading with them to slow down.

Tired and burned raw by the relentless sun, the two men literally collapsed into camp chairs after sunset Sunday night and slept there until Monday morning. The pace of the last few days had taken its toll on both Davis and Kool, and the strain of the ordeal was showing on the faces of their wives. Each of the previous weekday mornings, when Davis had left the camp for work, the Kools and Lois had scheduled the remainder of the day so that one of them was always standing watch over the whale. Their vantage point was an unshaded promontory from which the sentries repeatedly scanned the bay with binoculars to make sure the calf wasn't harassed by curious boaters, and to reassure themselves that the baby hadn't died or fled from the cove. The events of the past week had been physically and emotionally exhausting for everyone and, in spite of their efforts, there was a growing suspicion that the calf's condition was worsening. When Davis walked stiffly down to the skiff with a bucket of herring that morning, he realized the situation couldn't continue.

"I knew then she was sick – critically sick. I also knew there was no way I could keep feeding her – there was no way I could stay there indefinitely. I could see she was very dependent. I needed some direction."

But it wasn't without some misgivings – a feeling of loss – that Davis phoned a friend, Dr. Murray Newman, one of the directors of the Vancouver Aquarium.

CHAPTER 4

A Gambler's Chance

Davis couldn't have shaken the Vancouver Aquarium more if he'd planted a bomb in its midst.

"You've got a what? You're doing what?" Newman called disbelievingly into the phone. "Hold on a minute, Bill. I don't know whether you're just pulling my leg or not, but I'm going to put this call on the conference line so that my assistant can also hear what you're saying."

At that point Davis couldn't have cared less what kind of line he was put on just as long as Newman didn't hang up. He could hear the electronic clicks in the background as the connection was being changed in Vancouver. Although it didn't take more than a few seconds for the call to be transferred, it was long enough for Davis to realize just how tired he had become during the last week. It occurred to him he hadn't given his family or himself much thought since the whale had appeared. He was silently vowing to change that situation when Newman's voice toned over the receiver again.

"Can I get that story from the top again? You say you have a whale and that you've been hand-feeding it for a week?"

"That's only part of the story," Davis answered. "It has been shot and has a couple of other wounds as well as pock marks and a hair-like weed all over its skin. It's not swimming well, either."

Davis paused, hoping his story wasn't being considered just a prank call that was making a dull Monday a little more interesting for the aquarium directors.

"Look," he said, "I'm in a desperate situation. This whale is sick – deathly sick – as well as dependent for its food. I need some help."

"Are you sure it's a whale? Could you have mistaken it? Are you sure it's not something like a dolphin?" Newman asked.

"I'm sure," Davis said wearily. "I've got pictures. I've been fishing this coast for more than twenty years; I know what a killer whale looks like."

After accepting the story as at least possible Newman asked some more questions about the whale's size and its condition and then said he'd make the trip to see the calf. He never did make the journey but not because he didn't believe Davis – though he did retain a professional scepticism – but because of other circumstances.

Newman believed that as long as the story retained even a grain of possible accuracy it would have to be checked, and checked fast. A sick whale, especially one that was being fed by hand, was probably close to taking its last breath. It was with that thought in mind that he phoned Dr. Michael Bigg, co-ordinator of killer whale research at the Pacific Biological Station in Nanaimo – a town within several hours' drive of the whale calf's reported position.

Although Bigg suspected it was the same killer whale he'd seen in Nanaimo a month earlier he wanted to make sure. He contacted Federal Fishery officer Joe Fielding who was stationed at Campbell River. It turned out Fielding and Davis had been friends for many years but Fielding wasn't aware of a sick or stranded killer whale anywhere near Campbell River.

"But you can believe Davis. If he says he's got a killer whale, well then that's what he's got," Fielding told Bigg.

Still not satisfied, Bigg phoned Davis's office at the mill. It came as a surprise to Davis when Bigg identified himself and started asking another round of questions about the whale calf.

"I thought things had been arranged and settled with Dr. Newman," Davis recalled of the incident, "but half an hour after I made the call to Newman, Bigg phoned and asked the questions all over again. And I'd no sooner hung up the phone after that conversation when Fielding called, wanting to know why I hadn't called him first. I felt bad but explained that I'd been searching for people with a medical knowledge of whales."

During the afternoon Lois had watched as a Federal Fisheries officer motored a skiff into the inside bay, made one circuit of the cove, and left, apparently without seeing the calf.

After work Davis lounged in a camp chair outside the campers, following the short but sweaty drive from the mill. The last phone call he had received, about 2:00 that afternoon, was from Bigg, who said he would drive to the bay and meet Davis at the boat ramp between 5:00 and 6:00. Since they were camped beside the ramp Davis saw no reason to hurry dinner. He'd already decided to save the whale's herring so that he'd have some food with which to lure the calf to the boat when Bigg arrived.

Davis was never fully aware that his one call for help not only caused a stir of excitement along the island and the lower British Columbia mainland, but that it rang phones across the nation.

For Bigg, nestled amid the paperwork clutter in his cool basement office, the afternoon had been a long, frantic session of phone calls. After verifying the whale report as much as he could without seeing the animal himself, he phoned Sealand, an oceanarium in Victoria. Operations manager, Angus Matthews, took the call but asked Bigg to hold off on any action until Sealand's proprietor, Bob Wright, could be located.

Wright had just returned, tired, from a week-long fishing holiday at the north end of the island. It was well past noon when he walked past his secretary into his office that overlooked the forest of masts at Oak Bay Marina. After looking at the stack of paperwork piled on his desk he called gruffly for a cup of coffee and told his secretary not to put any calls through. Fifteen minutes later he hollered through his glass-panelled door for another cup of the afternoon's life-blood, but got no answer. Looking at his watch he realized his secretary had left for the weekly management meeting, so he resigned himself to getting his own coffee.

He had just placed the steaming cup on the right-hand side of his desk, and was drawing up his chair to sit down, when Matthews shoved open the door. Wright's stocky frame never even hit the padded chair before

Matthews' message brought him back to an upright position.

"For crud sake, what the hell would a killer whale be doing in Menzies Bay – being hand-fed of all things? Are you sure it's a whale and not some Stellar sea lion?"

"I'm not sure of anything – I don't even know where Menzies Bay is," Matthews said. "I got the report from Bigg. He's in his office now waiting for you to call him back. I'll be at Sealand if you turn up anything."

Wright's attitude of disbelief didn't surprise Matthews. In fact he was as doubtful of the third-hand report as his employer was. During the past ten years Sealand had become the unofficial marine branch of the Society for the Prevention of Cruelty to Animals and had been called on hundreds of times to rescue and nurse stranded marine animals. During that period Sealand staff had lost count of the number of reported whale strandings that turned out to have been nothing more than a seal or sea lion sunning itself. Although each report was checked and acted upon by the rescue team, it was never done without a certain amount of scepticism.

Enough of Wright's suspicion had been erased though, after the return call to Bigg, for him to charter a seaplane for the 200-mile trip to look at the whale. Wright also cancelled a flight, or at least made arrangements for one of his fishing partners of the previous week not to be on a scheduled flight.

Dr. Jay Hyman, one of the foremost aquatic veterinarians in North America, and the consulting veterinarian to the New York Aquarium, was more than a little surprised when two airline employees barred his entrance into the small plane leaving Victoria for Seattle. His protests – explanations that he had to make a connection in Seattle for his final flight to New York – were lost in the increasing whine of the accelerating plane engines. Just when he was getting angry enough to do battle with the two men, Oak Bay Marina manager, Wayne Wagner, drove up beside the aircraft and signalled Hyman to get into the car. Wagner told Hyman the story of the whale report during the drive back to the marina, stressing that it had been Wright's idea to have the veterinarian hauled off the plane. Hyman began to laugh.

"If you'd been a couple of minutes later we might have had a police escort, but it wouldn't have been to the marina," he said, remembering his heated exchange with the airline employees.

It was late afternoon by the time the plane circled and landed at the marina. The wind had shifted to an evening offshore breeze so that the seaplane was able to land within a few feet of Wright and Hyman who were waiting at the fuel float, stationed at the outermost edge of the marina dock complex. In less than a minute the men were aboard and the craft taxied towards the mouth of the bay so the pilot could turn the plane around and take off facing the breeze. The aircraft touched down in Nanaimo Harbour, about halfway along in the northward flight, to take Bigg aboard.

After the return phone call by Wright, Bigg had contacted Federal Fisheries Minister Romeo LeBlanc to get permission to capture the whale calf should it need extensive and prolonged treatment. When he clambered aboard the plane he apologized for being the bearer of bad news.

"I tried to contact you at the marina before you left but I was too late. I guess the flight thus far has been for nothing – LeBlanc's office has refused to issue a permit.

In fact they went as far as to order no one to even touch the whale.''

Wright's language at that point is beyond repeating, but, after having had his say about the federal political system, he confirmed with Hyman and Bigg before urging the pilot to continue the flight to Menzies Bay.

While in flight Bigg told Wright and Hyman the details of his conversation with LeBlanc. The information might have been news to Hyman, who was used to working under looser American laws, but it came as no surprise to Wright. He was aware that killer whales had become a politically hot potato in recent years – often both he and his oceanarium had found themselves in the middle of heated debates over killer whale issues. But he was not prepared for a direct order not to help a dying whale because it was not politically expedient to do so. Political expediency in this case could mean letting the killer whale die, unaided, in the wild instead of having it expire in captivity under treatment. Wright had a less-than-polite term for politics so practised.

His anger was not tempered by his growing feeling of apprehension – a feeling that they were on a wild goose chase to start with. That feeling was never stronger than when the plane reached Menzies Bay. The pilot banked the single-engined aircraft steeply and made a circular sweep so the men could get a better look at the cove. There was no whale. The plane circled again. This time the men saw a seagull and a seal frolicking in the water near the beach at the northern end. Still there was no whale. As the plane made its third, and what was to be its last circle of the bay, Hyman spotted a man in a small boat waving a hat over his head.

Davis had been relaxing in his camp chair when the aircraft made its first low circle. He was still expecting

Bigg to arrive by truck, not having heard otherwise, so he dismissed the plane as belonging to a sightseeing pilot. After it made a second pass he thought maybe the float plane carried Dr. Newman from Vancouver. He had pushed his waiting dinghy away from shore just in time to flag the aircraft down on its third sweep. The pilot dipped the aircraft's wings several times in answer to the hat waves and Davis watched the plane land before he started out to it in his dinghy.

When the passenger door of the aircraft opened and three strangers stepped out onto the pontoons Davis began to feel foolish. He knew Newman by sight, after having met him at a convention in Campbell River – none of these men was Newman. My God, he thought, I've flagged down a plane-load of complete strangers – they probably think I'm in trouble. He didn't know what to say so he just sat in his boat grinning. Bigg was the first to speak, but he got no further than uttering a few unintelligible words before stopping abruptly – he had forgotten Davis's name. It was Wright who punctured the awkward silence.

"Are you the man with the whale?" he asked simply.

"I'm the man who reported it, if that's who you're looking for."

"You're the man. I'm Bob Wright from Sealand. This is Michael Bigg, from the biological station at Nanaimo, and on my left is Dr. Jay Hyman, a veterinarian from New York. How do you usually go about finding this whale?"

"Climb aboard and I'll take you to it," Davis said.

As he motored the skiff away from the boom, where the pilot had moored the aircraft, Davis hoped desperately that the whale calf hadn't disappeared. He hadn't seen the calf since the morning and now he began to

wonder why the fisheries officer, who had cruised the bay earlier, hadn't seen it. He rolled down the sleeves of his shirt to protect his already sunburned arms, while the three visitors began shedding their light coats and unbuttoning their shirts. The descending sun always made the bay hot late in the day – especially during the current heat wave – but a faint breeze kept the temperature within reason this afternoon.

Once on the inside bay, Davis stopped the engine while everyone scanned the motionless water for a telltale ripple or the sight of a black fin. Nothing appeared. Several more minutes passed and Wright looked at his watch before continuing to scan the bay – they had slightly more than half an hour to find the whale and examine it before the plane would have to leave on its return trip. Because of the mirror effect of water during darkness, and a pilot's need of a high degree of visibility during landings, federal regulations forced float planes to land half an hour before dusk. Davis nervously tapped the throttle lever on the engine while Hyman and Bigg exchanged doubting glances.

"Where do you usually see it?" Wright asked suspiciously.

"It usually surfaces as soon as I enter the inner bay. I'm sure we'll see it soon," said Davis enthusiastically, if not convincingly.

More anxious minutes elapsed. Not even the seagull or seal, that had been playing before the plane landed, darted out to cut the silence or caused the water to ripple. Finally, under protest from Hyman, Davis started the engine in an effort to contact the whale calf – an act that would have been sure to scare away any normal killer whale. The men continued to scan the bay but with a mounting scepticism – in Wright's case, disbelief had reached its peak. Seconds later, as they were searching the water a hundred yards in the distance they were dampened by the fish-tainted mist of a killer whale's breath, that found its source less than two feet away from the skiff's port side. After a pause, which held lingering disbelief, Hyman was the first to speak.

"I don't believe it! Twenty years of research and it's all gone out the window. Killer whales just don't swim up to the sides of moving power boats."

Sensing that something was different, and seeing the strangers in the boat with Davis, the calf slowly moved to the stern of the skiff and refused to come alongside. Even when Davis tried to coax the baby with a herring, and then tried to put the boat broadside to it by using a spare paddle, the whale stayed beside the stern as if tethered by an unseen rope. Finally the ailing calf's hunger forced it to accept one of the fish, but it took the offering only from Davis's hand. It sounded with the fish between its jaws and when it resurfaced a short time later it ignored herring draped along the side of the boat near the strangers and waited patiently for another fish over the stern from Davis. The visitors leaned and twisted over Davis's shoulder, dipping the skiff at precarious angles to the water, to watch the spectacle. It was nearly half an hour before the baby took fish from the side of the boat and several more long minutes before it would roll on its side for a quick inspection by Hyman.

The veterinarian's face revealed as much as his words.

"The calf's condition is worse even than it looks – I'll stake my reputation on it." He avoided meeting Davis's eyes. When he spoke again, after a deep breath, his voice was noticeably quieter. "It'll be dead in two weeks at the latest if treatment isn't started immediately – we may already be too late."

Davis felt his throat tighten. He didn't look at the men nor did he look at the whale stretched out quietly along the side of the boat. He looked out over the stern, his gaze sweeping the rocky shoreline of the bay's northern corner. Dying rays of yellow-gold sunlight drew sparkling lines away from the boat across the water to the beach. A seagull flew across the bay through one of the shafts of light and emitted a high-pitched squawk before disappearing into the forest. Davis didn't see or hear anything else. His eyes ached and he felt tired. He was only partially aware of the other men discussing the calf's condition. It was Wright's voice that finally shook his head clear.

"There are a couple of choices. I think it only fair that you have the chance to make them. The whale will die if it's left here, and none of us are sure we can do anything for the calf, even if we do take charge of it. To treat it we'll have to move it to Victoria – Jay says the chances are a thousand-to-one against the calf surviving the journey. We'll try it only with your permission. If you decide you want the whale to stay in this bay I'll see you get all the herring you need to feed it until it dies."

It wasn't much of a decision. A thousand-to-one odds were still better than none.

"You try," were the only words Davis was able to choke up.

In making the decision to try to help the dying baby, Wright was knowingly contravening federal government orders. He could lose the permit to keep the male killer whale he already had at Sealand – in fact he could lose Sealand itself, a dream that had taken more than eight years to complete. But he knew that if he didn't try to help the whale – whatever the odds and whatever the cost – his own conscience wouldn't let him keep the oceanarium. Everything he had fought for, and come to believe in, was somehow personified in the dying whale calf.

*   *   *

When the aircraft landed in Nanaimo Harbour again Wright went ashore with Bigg to phone Matthews. By the time the plane landed in Oak Bay, just ahead of the dusk curfew imposed on float planes, the Sealand rescue team had assembled and almost finished loading equipment aboard several trucks.

Wright was in his office only moments before calling the team together for a briefing. It was a short and stormy session. The rescue was to be the largest and most delicate operation the team had ever undertaken, Wright told the men and women crammed into his office.

Despite reports by both Wright and Hyman the team members didn't fully believe they would find a whale just idly waiting to be rescued in some obscure bay up the coast, and they said as much. That didn't bother Wright, but when Matthews reminded him about the repercussions that might result from contravening a federal fisheries order, Wright slammed a fist onto the top of his desk.

"I'm a gambler and a damned good one. I'll worry about the government – you just make sure you save that whale." He signalled an abrupt end to the conversation by turning his back on Matthews before snatching up the telephone.

CHAPTER 5

Friends and Enemies

Davis twisted himself out of the overhead bunk, careful to crane his head away from the low ceiling, and quietly shut a sliding door that divided the sleeping area from the other sections of the camper. Lois was continuing to sleep through the pre-dawn. As Davis dressed in the darkness his wrist watch luminously stabbed out the time, 4:05 A.M., and the date, Tuesday, August 9. He switched on one of the battery-operated interior lights before igniting the propane stove. Several minutes later he slid a mug of coffee and a plate of toast beside his fishing hat that lay on one corner of the settee table.

Outside, the final silence before daybreak was touched only by the rhythm of the waves on the nearby beach. An ebb tide was gradually pulling water out of the bay, exposing long stretches of sand and rock shoreline previously under water. The harbour seals continued to sleep peacefully, draped over the rock outcroppings with just their fins or flippers reaching into the water to dissipate a build-up of body heat. Occasionally, several of the animals would squirm and roll themselves further down the rock to submerge fins that had been left dry by the retreating tide. They fully ignored the shallow breathing spouts of the baby whale. When they slid into the water shortly before dawn to hunt their first meal of the day they swam daringly close to the calf, almost bumping it as they streamed past. They knew instinctively that the whale was incapable of harming them and held it in contempt for its weakness.

Both the calf and Davis had slept fitfully, but for separate reasons. Davis knew what had to be done to save the baby but he was apprehensive about how the rescue would be accomplished. He knew little about Sealand, its rescue team or its methods. He worried about the possibility that the calf no longer had the inner resources to deal with the action and tension of a rescue operation. He was concerned that the weakening calf might be frightened into death before anyone could really begin to help it. As the morning hours grew closer to daylight, and to the planned rescue, he began wondering whether he'd really made the right choice by agreeing to the whale's capture. Just maybe, he thought, mother nature – who had been so neglectful in her care of the orphan – might have taken pity and cured the baby whale overnight. He knew better, though. He had often witnessed the finality of nature's decisions – with or without man's intervention.

The calf's sleep was tormented by the pain of dying and made fitful by its uncertainty of the past week's events. The baby whale was caught in a strange web. Having first learned that man was a cruel, unforgiving enemy, it was now forced to rely on these creatures for its life. Although the herring, and Davis's compassion, had restored the calf's will to live, it was only a matter of time before the spreading infections would grip the baby in the final stage of death. The whale was spending more and more time lying on the bottom of the bay, unable to keep itself at the surface for long periods. Its death was a process that brought compound defeat. The baby's weakening condition caused it to spout and breathe so shallowly that only a portion of the stale air was exhaled. The small amount of fresh air the baby took in allowed it to sound for just a short time before it was forced to resurface. The brief and frequent diving periods gave the calf minimal rest and further robbed it of diminishing energy.

At the same time that Davis had risen from bed, the eleven-member Sealand team had roused themselves from an hour-long nap. Jammed into two trucks – one of them a three-ton flatbed, rented specifically to transport the whale to Victoria – the team had arrived in Campbell River after driving most of the night. They stopped in the fishing-lumbering town long enough to recheck equipment lists and book into a hotel for a nap, before continuing the eight miles to Menzies Bay. Half an hour after waking, the team reached the bay and met with Davis, who had arranged to have the day off work. Wright and Hyman had left Victoria several hours before the rest of the team and had pushed Wright's sedan beyond all legal speed limits to reach the bay during the final hours of daylight the previous evening. They had kept sentry over the whale until after dusk when the last boatload of curiosity-seekers had finally left. Satisfied that the baby was safe for the night – at least from the ravages of man – they returned to the Campbell River hotel to get what sleep they could. For most of the crew, including Wright and Hyman, it would be fully forty-eight hours, and several emergencies later before they would be able to sleep again. Although actual rescue operations weren't slated to start until dawn, Hyman and Wright had stationed themselves at the whale's side an hour before the crew arrived during the shabby greyness of pre-dawn. They returned to Davis's beach-side camp as the trucks were backing onto the boat ramp.

While Wright talked quickly with Davis – putting to rest any fears he had that the calf might have expired overnight – the team began unloading the trucks of what looked strangely like the combined remnants of a logging camp and a landlocked fishing fleet. Lashed onto the flatdeck was a stack of fir beams of varying sizes. A sixteen-foot dinghy was wedged between the lumber and a tangle of iron pipe, fabric, chains, and sheepskin that was, in reality, the sling that would be used to lift and transport the calf to Victoria. Inside the dinghy an assortment of hand tools were scattered around a gasoline generator that would be used to power electric drills and saws, also stashed in the corners of the boat. The other truck, a crewcab pickup, looked at first glance like a fishing net that had sprouted wheels. But after the net had been unloaded, a pair of glass fibre skiffs became visible amid a clutter of lead fishing balls, inflatable buoys, cork floats, diving tanks and suits, yards of nylon line, an outboard motor, oars, anchors, and other oddities needed to make the rescue.

One of the skiffs was so laden with equipment that

when it was launched the gunwhales poked less than a hand's width above the surface of the water. The other dinghy, loaded almost as heavily with people, took the equipment skiff in tow and slowly motored around the shoal to the inside bay. Davis had led the way with Hyman and Wright in his boat. As the convoy entered the inner bay the team – still sceptical about finding a whale in the cove – got their first glimpse of the calf as it surfaced to follow Davis's boat. Davis purposely stopped his skiff in mid-bay, while the other two boats continued for the nearby shore. The three men in Davis's boat took on the task of keeping the calf's attention. It was a job made easier by a new development in the whale's behaviour – the calf would surface beside Davis whenever he slapped the palm of his hand against the water. While this was happening the crew members on shore began preparations to surround the whale with a semi-circle of net that would start and end at two separate points along the beach.

The sun was just rising behind the Quadra Island hills opposite the mouth of the bay – it wasn't yet visible but it stretched out the first hue of morning light – as the crew unloaded the last pieces of equipment onto the rocky beach at the northern corner of the bay. By the time the team had readied the nets, restacked them in the boat, and started laying them in position, the mists that had formed in the bay overnight had burned off, making way for the strengthening heat and glare of the naked sun.

Davis watched anxiously as the crew worked. He wasn't fully able to comprehend his fleeting feelings as the rescue work progressed. One moment he felt closed in by the aluminum confines of his skiff, as it drifted slowly and aimlessly near the shoreline, and he felt threatened by the quiet strangers sitting next to him. The preparations that the crew were making on the beach almost frightened him because, although he could see the work and workers, he didn't really understand the eventual use of the equipment or the manpower.

In another moment he felt hopeful – almost drunk with a feeling of good will – that despite the cruelty of some men he was struggling to reverse the wrongdoings of others. The fact that he had developed a bond – an intangible and unexplainable love that was being returned by the whale – served only to further confuse his emotions. It wasn't until months later that, with the understanding help of Lois, he was able to identify these feelings. And it wasn't until that time that he realized he wasn't alone in the alternate tides of despondency and elation that continued to grip him throughout that long day.

Bob Wright wasn't motivated by love but rather by compassion – a trait that ran hard aground on his sharply-honed sense of business. Wright was the epitome of the self-made man. With little more than dreams in his pockets he had built the largest and most modern marina complex in British Columbia and then extended his ownership and influence into almost a dozen other companies that stretched throughout the Canadian and American Pacific coast. Sealand, and several affiliate companies, remain as his only emotional excursion into the sober world of business.

His best judgement now told him to abort the rescue mission before his defiance of federal government orders became known and caused irreversible shock waves throughout his financial realm. That same sense reminded him doggedly that, although he was the only man in Canada to retain a federal government permit to capture a "healthy" whale as a mate for the male already in the oceanarium, any political boat-rocking would surely see that permit rescinded. Although the orphan that lay alongside the skiff was more dead than alive, Wright knew political or financial arguments had no rightful place in a decision of whether or not to continue helping the dying animal. He also knew his business sense would not be laid to rest by a mere emotional commitment. He would have to fight all the practical reasons why he shouldn't be involved because if the whale died in his care, his good judgement would be no consolation.

Jay Hyman was the one addition to the team who was expected to have a dramatic impact on the mission's success factor – to change the possibility of "she might live" to a definite "she will live." He had pioneered techniques of aquatic mammal medicine that had saved the lives of innumerable dolphins near his New York City home. As the consulting veterinarian to the New York Aquarium he had been called on to treat "no hope" cases involving seals, sea lions, and Beluga whales. His success rate was well-known, almost legendary. Yet it was he who had to break the news that the calf's chances of surviving the overland trip to Victoria were slim, almost non-existent.

Hyman was aware of his duties and of the mystical way in which medical doctors are regarded, whether they tend to humans or animals. He was also painfully aware of his shortcomings. Although he had treated many dolphins, the smaller look-alike cousin of the killer whale, he had had no experience with killer whales, nor had he ever been called upon to deal with an animal as different from others in its species as this one was. His practised eye could detect life draining from the whale, almost as if life were a vapour or liquid. The baby was dying in front of his eyes, of that much he was sure. But it was what he couldn't see or know – the internal damage and ebb and flow of will power, on which the baby now seemed to solely exist – that bothered him most. He knew it would take much more than he had to make the calf well again. It would take a miracle.

The calf needed little coaxing to stay beside the skiff, although about once every fifteen minutes it would slide below the surface and lay in the cool sand for several minutes to rest and escape the drying heat of the sun. Davis, Wright and Hyman took turns splashing water on its scarred, growth-infested skin while it lay along the surface on the shady side of the skiff. The three men, like the other rescue team members, had stripped down to shorts, hats, and sunglasses, and then rubbed each other down with a lotion to protect themselves against sunburn. Throughout the day most of the crew would alternately strip and dress again as they struggled first to escape the heat and then later to try to hide from the sun's skin-burning rays.

As the three men in Davis's boat kept the calf's attention, Matthews continued to direct the net-laying operation from shore. At twenty-five years of age the fair-skinned, blond-haired leader of the rescue team was one of the youngest members of the crew. But it wasn't his age that made Matthews look singularly out of place, it was his boyish good looks. He looked more like an aspiring movie actor on location than part of a whale rescue operation that was on the border of legal and political controversy. Despite his easy-going nature and quick, eye-squinting laugh, Matthews was a demanding leader, and the hand-picked rescue team moved

smoothly and precisely under his direction. Although he tried not to speculate about the calf's past or its uncertain future – his immediate and all-consuming task was to confine the baby and see it safely to Victoria – he couldn't help wondering why an animal so mistreated by man could still be so trusting of this fickle land creature.

The first part of the net-laying operation, which would confine the whale in a semi-circle of net stretched from shore, went quickly and without problems. The calf didn't seem to notice the net until it was halfway around an eventual 200-foot radius. And then, without warning, the calf slid into a shallow dive and started swimming slowly but determinedly toward the mass of webbing and the boat laying it. Warned by a series of frantic shouts the operators of the net-laying skiffs quickly shut off their outboard engines. The calf swam stiffly beneath the boats and the now still propellers to surface beside the net. It ran one of its side-protruding pectoral fins along several feet of the webbing before it turned to station itself ten feet away, but still within the confines of the net. It stayed submerged for several minutes, at first moving nothing except its tail in an effort to remain stationary. Then slowly it began to move its head from side to side as it further investigated the entwined cordage with sonar bounces.

As suddenly as it had left, the baby returned to Davis's skiff. Matthews waved the net-laying crew back into action, visibly relieved that the calf had chosen to swim back to the dinghy. His biggest fear had been that the whale – which showed the scars of having tangled with a net at some point during its short life – might either try to battle with the cord mesh or try to escape. Had the calf chosen either of the actions it would have forced the crew to pick up the net and start over – an agonizing waste of precious time.

Once the calf had repositioned itself beside the familiar dinghy it never again ventured out to investigate the continuing activities around it. As soon as the net-laying crew had completed its task and the baby had been restricted to a shallow area near the beach, Wright had one of the skiffs take him from Davis's boat to the shoreline where Matthews stood. Wright was becoming anxious about the number of curiosity-seekers filing into the bay. The calf was showing an increasing nervous reaction to the high-pitched engine whines and would often dive until the noise subsided. Both men were fearful that the whale's frightened dives were depleting it of already waning energy resources.

Matthews had just finished ordering two team members to station themselves in a skiff along the seaward side of the net when a glass fibre cruiser sped through the channel into the inner bay. The operator continued to push the boat at a fast pace until he came up beside the net, at which time he wheeled the cruiser around in a sharp turn before thrusting the engine into a high-speed reverse. The wash from the manoeuvre threatened to rip out the net anchors and Wright cursed. He gruffly ordered Matthews to take him out to the cruiser. As Matthews piloted the dinghy along the outside of the net, passing within fifty feet of the confined whale, Davis stood up in his skiff and waved his hands over his head.

"I know the guy," he shouted. "He won't hurt the whale."

Neither Wright nor Matthews heard or saw Davis.

The man who walked to the stern of the cruiser, after heaving a large salmon within ten feet of the whale calf, was slender, chocolate-tanned and in his early thirties.

Wright and Matthews learned almost immediately that his name was Grant Thompson. He was ambitious, physically tough, and lacked only diplomacy among the characteristics that singled him out as a leader. In fact, he was the crew foreman for the MacMillan Bloedel log booming ground set along the southwestern shore of the inner bay. He dealt daily with tough men in a job that demanded cock-sureness much more than it did the weak-jawed front of diplomacy. Wright could sense, before they came alongside the cruiser, that the man wasn't to be challenged.

Thompson, like Davis, fished the nearby waters with a regularity that was seldom threatened by weather. He had often witnessed the passage and antics of killer whales and he was almost subordinately respectful of their power and prowess. He had been among the first boatloads of curious people that now daily gathered around the calf, but his curiosity had turned to concern as he watched the baby whale visibly weaken during the past week. He was unaware of the commitment that Sealand had made to the calf and considered the mass of equipment – especially the net – a further threat to the baby's life.

Wright regarded Thompson as an equal threat.

"We'd appreciate it if you didn't feed the whale too much," Wright said, failing his best shot at checking his temper. "And the next time you come in, if you could do it a little slower it would help us out a whole lot."

Further irritated by the remarks, Thompson spat out a volley of words that lost none of their sharpness in the verbal rapid-fire.

"And who the hell are you, mister? I'm not doing anything or going anywhere until you guys pack all this stuff and get out of here. I want this whale left alone. And when you're finished you're going to stick around just long enough to tell me what you thought you were going to do with the whale."

Familiar with a variety of misconceptions about killer whales, and about their rescue team, Matthews and Wright had expected at least one bout of abuse during the rescue operation. Yet this confrontation had all the earmarks of becoming something substantially more than just a shouting match. Thompson didn't know it yet but one call from him to the proper authorities could not only serve to stop the entire rescue but would have the bay overrun with federal fisheries officers and Mounties – a prospect that Matthews was not eager to face. For the first time during his eight years at Sealand he was able to outshout Wright and he also managed to make himself heard above the din of Thompson's anger. Carefully and slowly he wound the argument down to a discussion. After half an hour he had convinced Thompson that the rescue team was working for the dying calf and was doing everything possible to save its life.

Buoyed by the outcome of the talks, Wright asked off-handedly if the logger knew where the team could charter a boat capable of lifting the whale from the water. Thompson gave the question such quiet, lengthy consideration that Wright was about to ask the question again when the logger finally spoke.

"I think I can do better than a boat – I can't promise anything just yet, but the company has a self-powered barge with a crane. If you give me some men I'll try to see what I can do. While I'm at it, is there any other equipment you might need."

The wind-shift change in Thompson's attitude was so abrupt, and so complete, that neither Wright nor Matthews could speak for a moment. During the pause Wright pierced Thompson's hard shell, mentally probing into the core of the logger's personality. He was able to make an immediate evaluation of the man standing in front of him. Wright's ability to size a person in mid-track – and to evaluate situations almost as rapidly – had been his one avenue to business success. Some people called it a sixth sense. Wright had no name for it but he clung tenaciously to its inevitable wisdom.

"I like the cut of your jib, Thompson," he said with a sudden boisterousness. "Follow us. I'll introduce you to the crew and see that you get the men you need."

The logger took four of the team's strongest members aboard his cruiser. As he motored toward the booming ground Wright and Matthews climbed into the pick-up truck and left the bay behind in a swirl of dust.

CHAPTER 6

A Daring Plan
and a Prayer

The gravel-road dust billowed through the open truck windows, choking the air. But neither Wright nor Matthews made an effort to close the windows during the half-mile drive to the highway – it was too hot in the truck, even with the windows down. Once on the paved highway the men rode in comparative comfort toward Campbell River. Matthews was making the trip to buy supplies and equipment needed for the advanced stages of the rescue, while Wright was going to monopolize at least one of the town hotel's phones to confirm arrangements for the calf's arrival in Victoria. Matthews had also undertaken the responsibility for a lunch delivery to the crew – most of whom hadn't eaten since the previous day.

The team that remained at Menzies Bay found out all too painfully that the needs of the whale calf were given absolute priority – even over lunch. There hadn't been enough room for the food aboard the first boat that left the boat ramp with the special delivery of newly purchased hardware, and the skipper of the second boat simply forgot it when he sped away from the landing. It was after 5:00 that evening before the crew was able to tear into their first and only meal of the day.

When Wright and Matthews returned from town it was to scan a scene of hustling activity. Not only had Thompson secured the crane barge but he had enlisted two of MacMillan Bloedel's pudgy, steel boom boats, which were now growling around the bay with logs in tow for the construction of a floating pond net. The prolonged heat wave had closed all island logging operations several weeks previously, which in turn had closed the booming ground, except for a maintenance crew of four men, who had nothing to do but wait for the unused machinery to break down. When the men learned of Thompson's involvement with the rescue they also volunteered to help. It was these men whom Wright could see sawing the logs that the boom boats were tugging from the southern end of the bay to the northern corner. By the time the last half of the rescue crew had finished their late lunch, the loggers and the other half of the Sealand team had completed construction of the sixty-six-foot floating log square. By 6:00 a special net, which had four connected sides and a bottom that reached fourteen feet below the water, had been nailed to the logs, completing the pond.

Throughout the afternoon the loggers had taken a good-natured ribbing from the rescue team. They were repeatedly shown how a sailor would undertake a specific task – the underlying implication, of course, was that the loggers had a lot to learn. It was a natural rivalry between landsmen and seamen. For most of the day the rescue team maintained an upper hand in the contest, but that began to change at 7:00 as the team embarked on the trickiest part of the rescue.

The most worrisome part of containing a killer whale for the rescue crew had always been the risky man-oeuvre involved in transferring the whale from the capture nets into the net pond. The pond itself was designed to produce a much more controlled confinement than the beach side nets, which were susceptible to damage from fast-flowing tides. A whale confined to a pond was easily accessible to both emergency and continuing medical treatment. The normal method of transfer was to gather one end of the capture net, forcing the whale to the opposite end, and at the same time reducing the area of confinement. When the whale had been herded into a small area of the capture net, the mesh would be butted to one end of the floating pond. The corresponding end of the pond net would be dropped, sometimes a log temporarily removed, and the whale coaxed from one area to the other. If the whale became frightened in mid-transfer it could easily push aside the overlapping nets and escape. It was a delicate procedure but during many rescue operations the technique had been polished to the point where the crew believed no alternative method of making the transfer could be better.

It took Thompson and Davis to explode that belief. Rescue leaders were sceptical when Thompson approached them with what he claimed was an easier and far less risky approach to the transfer. He wanted to drive one of the boom boats on top of one side of the pond to force the log to sink under the boat. The capture net could be placed at least part way into the pond, he reasoned, and the whale could then be emptied out at the same time the boom boat was backed away.

It wouldn't work, he was told. There was too much danger of breaking up the log pond and, besides, the whale would sense the log beneath it and struggle in the net, which could cause unnecessary injuries. The discussion might have been left at an impasse had Davis, having overheard the conversation, not suggested that he simply call the calf from one net to the other after Thompson cleared the way by submerging the log barrier. Matthews wouldn't have considered the scheme had Wright not gone ashore to make more telephone calls to try to get proper authorization to help the baby whale. It was Wright who had conceived the idea of the rescue team and its procedures. He was justifiably proud of its success record and jealously guarded control of its operation. When Matthews finally said Yes to the daring plan it was with the knowledge that his superior would have quashed it at the outset. If Thompson had any second thoughts he didn't let on.

Davis wished he could have withdrawn his suggestion as soon as he had made it. He had never denied himself the pleasure that came from knowing there was a special bond between himself and the dying calf. And he revelled, to a certain extent, in the knowledge that other people recognized that this bond existed. Yet as he guided his skiff to the opposite end of the pond from where the calf was to enter the enclosure, he began to seriously doubt the extent of that relationship. The team had been working for more than twelve hours to rescue the baby and Davis couldn't now recall a single incident during that time where the baby had shown a special preference for him over the others.

He had sunk into his own thoughts so deeply that he carried out his task mechanically, not watching or thinking about the crew around him. He tied both the bow and stern of the skiff to the log that formed the perimeter of the far end of the pool and leaned out of the boat and over the log. Thompson had already submerged the log on his side of the pond, although the crew, struggling to overlap the nets as a primary precaution, had not finished their task when Davis brought his hand against the water in two signal slaps. Before anyone realized what was happening the calf wrenched free of the net and was swimming inside the pond.

The crescendo of shouts and cheers was almost lost to the gutteral noise of Thompson's diesel-powered boom boat, as he backed it off the log. Three of the four other loggers deftly leapt to the boat's steel deck as the boat was swung around to head for the booming ground. There were two more transfers to make and Thompson, now an integral part of the rescue team, was on his way to make sure they happened on schedule.

Tired, and further burnt by the sun that continued to heat the bay, Davis was not ready for the emotional wound that happened minutes after the calf had been transferred. Despite an order by Matthews to stop the minimal feedings that had been offered to the calf throughout the day – an order that rested on the common sense of keeping the calf's stomach as empty as possible so it could more easily deal with the trauma of the overland trip – Davis had managed to negotiate two final herring remnants for the baby. The rescue team perched themselves around the floating pond, watching the whale and Davis while they waited for Thompson to return with the crane barge. Davis slapped a large piece of fish on the glassy surface of the enclosure. The calf, lying idly at the surface in the middle of the pond, turned slowly and glided towards the sound. It kept moving, barely causing a ripple in the still water, until it was within five feet of Davis. It stopped, lifted its head out of the water to look at Davis with one eye, and emitted a short squeal before turning and swimming away. Davis tried a half-dozen more times to hand-feed the baby before accepting the rejection and throwing the fish slices into centre pool. He lit a cigarette and held it between shaky fingers as he squatted on the log and watched the whale for several minutes. The rest of the crew moved and congregated in small groups while Hyman remained silently perched on the log beside Davis. He was the only person who saw the two small tears slide down from under Davis's sunglasses.

By the time Thompson had wrestled the crane into position, Wright had returned from Campbell River and his second spate of phone calls. This time there was good news – Federal Fisheries Minister Romeo LeBlanc had reversed his earlier decision and had issued a permit to capture the dying whale calf. On the official records it was reported that the second decision followed a recommendation by Michael Bigg that the calf be confined and retained for treatment. In reality the first decision was reversed only after several pleading phone calls by Bigg to LeBlanc's staff and as many calls by Wright. During the last conversation Wright succinctly pointed out how badly the government office would look during a court battle which he was willing to initiate, and just how politically inconvenient that legal battle might prove to be.

Matthews split his crew in half. One section of the team stayed at the pool to ready the calf for the next transfer while the other members were detailed to build

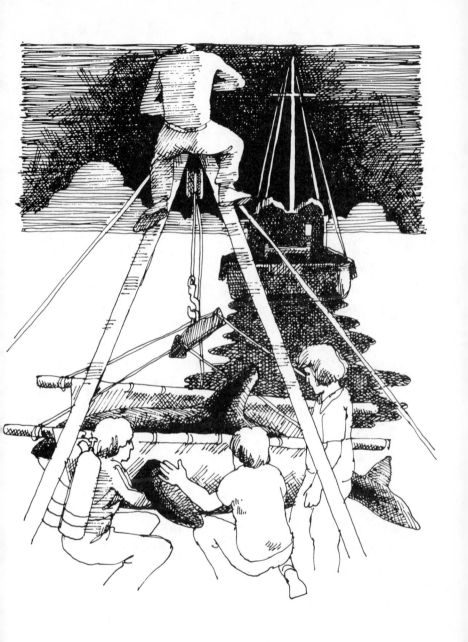

a form onto the back of the flatdeck truck that would hold the calf's sling. Thompson had already divided his crew – two men to work with him and two others to ready a shoreside crane that would be used to make the final transfer of the whale and sling to the truck. Working now under legal sanction the tired team redoubled its efforts.

As belly bands and a tail noose were slid around the baby to keep her still while divers worked the special sling around it, Davis felt a compulsion to leave the scene for the close comfort of his camper. The calf was making no secret of its fright. It squirmed continuously within the crane-tethered bonds of the bands and vocalized panic-stricken squeals between short, anxious breaths. Davis had witnessed about as much as he could stomach when Wright touched his shoulder.

"I think maybe we share the same feelings," Wright confessed. "I can take just about anything but I'll never get used to the sight and sounds of whales in pain or fear. Let's see if there's any coffee in that camper of yours."

Davis mutely nodded his agreement. They clambered into Davis's skiff and left the sights and sounds behind in a whine of engine noise. Lois met the two men at the ramp, where she had been watching the rescue. Davis told her of the events up to that point as the three walked to the camper. She left the men outside and returned a short time later with coffee which Davis and Wright drank silently in the shade of the alder trees. It was molten shade of a late summer evening, not like the crisply defined shadows that filtered through the leafy trees under the noon-day sun. Even though the bank of trees acted as a sound barrier between the beach and the campsite, the men could still hear the snorty growl of diesel engines as they were accelerated in short spurts. The most audible sound was the complaining squeal of pulleys as wire hausers were dragged through them. Occasionally a distance-muffled shout would tumble through the trees to land on the men's ears. Both men had given themselves over to private thoughts about the calf – fears and hopes – but it was Wright who first assaulted the privacy.

"They're very forgiving animals – often much more forgiving than people. Give it at least a couple of weeks before you condemn the relationship."

"I'm just trying to think of everything it's feeling now," Davis said, looking up from a detailed study of the bottom of his empty coffee mug. "I'm not sure I could handle the fright and confusion it's faced today. I guess I feel helpless. Before, I could help it – at least I thought I could. Now all I can do is stand by and watch and I can't even do that."

"We're doing everything we can," Wright assured him of Sealand's efforts. "No one can make any promises, but that's one plucky whale. No other killer whale could have survived the things that are already behind this calf. You've got to believe that the worst is over. Hyman has already shot a couple of needles full of antibiotics into the calf."

"I suppose you're right," Davis answered. It's just that things are moving so fast now that it's going to take me a little while to file everything away and get used to it all."

"Maybe a walk will help," Wright said, stretching his short, stocky frame out of the camp chair.

The tide had turned during the afternoon and left only a short stretch of beach that the men could walk along. They walked back and forth several times, catching glimpses of the continuing rescue operation a quarter of a mile away. Finally Davis suggested that they should return to the action – that regardless of their own feelings it was still the baby's hour of greatest need.

They returned to the inner bay in time to tie the skiff to the stern of the self-powered crane barge as it rumbled into a slow pace across and down the bay toward the booming ground. Along the blunt, slab-sided bow of the boat an A-frame crane angled up twenty feet over the water in front of the vessel. Less than three feet above the water the whale calf hung quiet in the soft confines of the sheepskin-lined sling. A boom boat had been sent ahead to clear a passage by slamming open secret gates in the interlocking log corrals that formed the booming ground.

It was dark as the barge moved noisely through the channels. Thompson picked his way carefully, stabbing the light of a search lamp through the darkness to reveal the watery path that twisted through the booms. Shortly after 9:00 P.M. the barge was tied, bow on, to a stubby pier that jutted out from the shore about halfway along the booming area. A massive A-frame – constructed of three six-foot-diameter logs – reached skyward more than a hundred feet over the end of the dock. Nearby the engine that powered the crane's cables through a six-block pulley system, pounded out a noisy uneven beat as it waited to be accelerated into action. The entire rig fairly wreaked power, yet Matthews wasn't sure whether the crude looking equipment was to be trusted.

"Are you sure this can take the weight of the whale?" Matthews asked Thompson as the cables were connected and the whale's weight taken off the barge crane. "You realize the whale probably weighs 800 pounds, and the wet sling at least that much again. Are you sure you can do it? The animal could move or twitch, which could make the weight 3,000 pounds."

Thompson eyed Matthews with disbelief before he answered.

"Look, this crane is designed for lifting 280 tons of logs at a single crack and I just hope you guys can get the slack out of the cables."

And Thompson was right. Even with five men dangling from the cable to add weight, the whale almost floated up the fifteen-foot height that she was lifted to. Although the transfer from the barge to the truck went well it took time, as did all other facets of the rescue. By the time the calf's sling was secured to the special railings built onto the back of the flatdeck truck, and the baby had been wetted and rubbed with a layer of lanolin to preserve skin moisture, it was midnight.

On the back with the calf were five rescue team members and six five-gallon reservoirs of water needed to wet the whale during the journey. The driver was armed with a map showing the all-night service stations along the route where the containers could be refilled.

On the dock Davis watched until the truck and whale were out of sight. And when he could see them no more he stood quietly and listened to the vehicle as it was shifted through the gears on the highway that ran south a half-mile away. He listened until the sound was lost to the waves washing against the dock pilings below his feet and then he said a silent prayer for the whale that had become his friend.

CHAPTER 7

A Call to Action

Wright made a detailed inspection of the sling as well as the framing that suspended it above the truck deck, and patted and talked to the calf encouragingly before speeding his car toward Campbell River. He left the bay several minutes ahead of the truck and reached the townsite a little more than five minutes later, a full half-hour before the truck passed through the town. At the town hotel he went unchallenged as he ran into the lobby and snatched a telephone from the receiving desk.

Although work had finished at one end of the rescue it was just going to begin at the other end in Victoria. Oak Bay Marina manager Wayne Wagner answered Wright's call in a sleepy monotone. It was 12:30 A.M. and

Wagner had squared himself off early the previous evening to get a full night's sleep – an act that hadn't become in danger of developing into a habit during recent weeks. He groaned wearily as Wright's voice spiked through the receiver.

Wright outlined what would have been a colossal undertaking even under normal circumstances and then put an impossible four-hour deadline on his demands. Wagner, although one of Wright's newest management employees, had worked long enough under his boss to know that any attempt at argument would be futile. As a matter of habit he penned the highlights of the orders onto a pad beside the telephone. But it wasn't until he was off the phone, and had a chance to reread the scribbled notes in reference to the deadline, that he really began to realize the magnitude of his chores. His first decision was not to suffer the load alone. He arranged to meet Les Wood, the manager of Sealand's sister aquarium in Victoria. However it wasn't Wood's managerial capabilities but his specialized knowledge of marine engineering that endeared him to the operation at this point.

Wright's orders were a surprise more in terms of timing than of content. Wagner had an almost identical copy of the demands on his desk at the marina, which had been laid there by Wright, before he made the final trip by car to Menzies Bay. The plan, re-affirmed by Wright Tuesday afternoon, had originally scheduled the whale calf to arrive in Victoria about noon Wednesday but the concerted efforts of the rescue crew, and invaluable help and expertise of Thompson and the loggers, had pushed the expected arrival ahead by almost eight hours. Connected to the original slate of orders – as well as to the telephone re-affirmation of those orders – was a sizable "if." Wagner was to act on the plan only if he heard from Wright, and that contact would be made if the federal fisheries didn't have the operation seized, and if the calf lived long enough to be placed on the truck.

Early in the rescue Hyman had warned Wright about the dangers of placing the dying calf in any of the pools at Sealand. It would take days and weeks of medical examinations and analysis to determine all the ailments from which the calf was suffering, he told Wright. Some of the problems, such as parasites, fungus growths, and infections might be highly contagious and could convert the oceanarium into a floating morgue overnight. The baby, he said, would have to be isolated from all other marine life, preferably in a shallow enclosure which would allow the calf to be easily recovered if it sank.

Wright had anticipated the problems and launched into a solution-finding mission before leaving for Menzies Bay. In fact, what he had done was to walk into the office of one of Victoria's more elegant hotels and ask the owner if he didn't have accommodations for a guest that was to be visiting Sealand. Oak Bay Beach Hotel proprietor Bruce Walker apologized profusely but replied that all his rooms had been taken. When Wright said a lack of rooms was of no importance, that his friend would rather sleep at the end of the back garden near the beach, Walker began to suspect something unusual about Wright's guest. It was then that Wright told Walker of the whale calf and Sealand's need for a pool – exactly like the one at Oak Bay Beach Hotel – that could be used for the whale's recovery.

If Walker had any better instincts he didn't react to them. Only later did he realize how badly an adverse situation, such as the whale dying in his pool, could have affected his livelihood. As it happened the ancient drain-and-fill pool had been closed to public use by the health department two weeks previously. The absence of any filters, and the need for the pool to be drained and refilled from the ocean to be kept clean, had put it on the department's list of the ten most unwanted facilities. They had originally ordered the pool's closure several years before, but the owners of the hotel at that time chose to ignore the order and they kept it operating. After his purchase of the hotel, Walker, not knowing about the health order, had also kept the facility available to hotel patrons. He drained the pool the same day a zealous health officer delivered a copy of the eight-year-old closure order. There was nothing, however, in the provincial statutes that would forbid a killer whale from using the pool.

The hotel itself was a sprawling, tudor-style structure designed to appeal to the asthetic sense of Oak Bay as the last British stronghold in North America. Although visiting Britishers often remarked that Victoria and Oak Bay were more British than any part of the United Kingdom – and that British immigrants to the area often moved at least one peg higher than their previous status on the English system of class distinction–the municipality was nonetheless steeped in the traditions of the old country. The hotel was as much a part of the scene as walking canes, tweed suits, and afternoon tea. From the front the hostelry looked like a grand mansion, so much so that its commercial use in the middle of a fashionable residential area was hardly noticed. And the back yard, which swept gently down to the sea, was the dream of any English country gardener. On the left seaward corner sat an unused boathouse, and next to that was the pool, which took advantage of a sea-washed nook in

the rock outcropping that leaned up the bank away from the beach. Concrete walls had been poured into place along the gaping hole near the beach and partially along each side, to complete a pool that had a natural shallow end and a man-made deep section.

When Wagner and Wood arrived at the pool, only a couple of the entrance and floodlights were on outside and subdued light stretched through a short bank of windows along the seaward side of the main floor, created by the night lamps in the lobby. An hour later guest room lights began winking on; just a few at first and then more until all but a couple of rooms showed lights. Guests peeked nervously beneath window shades for a short time and then, realizing the noise outside wasn't going to stop, they pushed open windows to shout questions at the workers. They were told quickly and politely that the workmen were preparing the pool to house an injured killer whale. Some of the guests pulled on clothes and wandered down to the pool to get a closer look, and some even stayed to lend a hand, while others continued to watch from the bird's-eye vantage points of their windows. Through it all the hotel received only one complaint – an elderly gentleman inflicted with an acute hearing loss asked bitterly why he hadn't been awakened to watch the spectacle.

With precious little time remaining to make ready for the whale calf's arrival, Wagner and Wood gave little thought to the oddities of human nature. To be ready meant cleaning and patching the ancient and unfilled pool. Before that could be done spotlights had to be erected to illuminate the area and that meant the pool area had to have a supply of electricity. Wagner was shocked after he had completed a half-hour of phone calls that began at 1:30 A.M. Not one of the business owners or tradesmen that he called had even uttered a curse and, without exception, after he had explained the urgency of the situation, everyone contacted was either on the site or working in their own shops half an hour after receiving the call.

By 3:00 that Wednesday morning a score of men busily attended their assigned tasks under the penetrating light of the spot lamps. Wood took delivery of three pumps – two electric machines and a gasoline pump to act as a back-up unit – and immediately began designing and building a pumping system that would keep the pool full despite the hundred or so leaks in its walls. Conscripted Sealand personnel began the laborious task of cleaning the pool and patching as many leaks as they could before zero hour. A whistling tradesman had quickly cut and installed steel posts in a thirty-foot arc around the pool and was beginning to stretch the first section of vinyl-coated mesh fencing that would be needed to keep back the expected crowds of the curious.

At 3:30 A.M. Dr. Alan Hoey, consulting veterinarian to Sealand, was put on standby alert. He in turn put a half-dozen of his own medical team on standby and then alerted one of Victoria's two hospital laboratories to be ready to receive and analyze samples of the whale's blood. He then drove to the pool to wait.

One of the more unusual companies that Wagner had phoned was that of a sign maker. Signs weren't as urgent as pumps and medical teams but if the crowds were to be kept off the finely mowed expanse of lawn and out of the manicured flower beds, they were a necessity.

"Do you like the colour blue?" asked the sign painter,

with amazing coherence, considering the time of night and odd circumstances of the call.

"At the moment I'd love any colour – hot pink, you name it, and it'll be my passion's desire I'm sure," Wagner answered.

"Well look, we've got a bunch of signs we were doing in a blue background for another job, but if you don't mind the colour we'll cut them up, letter them, and have them to you in a few hours. Mind you, they'll still be a bit tacky but they should be completely dry by the end of the day."

With that the painter hung up before Wagner could answer back, but by 4:00 he was carefully staking a truck load of signs into appropriate places along the edge of the parking lot and down the walkway.

The most amazing accomplishment had to be the installation of a poolside phone. The British Columbia Telephone Company, wrestling with a provincial population, whose numbers had exploded past the company's wildest growth expectations, had not been renowned for fast service in recent years. In fact most customers ordering a new phone installation were put on a six- to eight-week waiting list. Wagner had laughed and called Hoey a dreamer when the veterinarian asked to have a phone included on the list of chores that night.

"It's every bit as important as water in the pool," Hoey insisted. "If the Sealand team has to delay one minute in reporting any kind of abnormality to the medical team, the calf could be dead before anyone could even start to help it. Communication has got to be the strongest link in the chain of recovery for this animal. We haven't got the manpower to have medical people at poolside twenty-four hours a day. We need a telephone."

"You don't have to tell me," Wagner said defensively. "It's B.C. Tel that's going to have to be sold on the urgency of the situation. Why don't you give them a call and see what you can do."

Hoey was prepared for a stormy session of explanations and arguments but he'd only gotten halfway through a breathless spiel when the repair technician on nightshift interrupted and said, "We'll see to it immediately, sir," and hung up. An hour and a half later Hoey made his first test call from the poolside phone.

"It's not an entirely legal hook-up, but I don't think anyone here is going to complain," the B.C. Tel man said with a wink before he drove away.

While the phone was being installed Wagner, Wood, and the other Sealand members at the site were carefully adjusting pumps and intake hoses and at the same time logging the amount of time it took to fill the pool. Later they recorded the time required to drain the enclosure. Their findings would be invaluable if the whale calf sank and the pool had to be drained in order to administer medical attention. It would also be necessary to know how fast pumps could refill the pool.

It was 5:00 when the crew finally sat down to a round of coffee in the gathering warmth of a vivid orange sunrise. Wagner couldn't help smiling as he looked around at the odd assortment of tradesmen. They were more than just tradesmen, he thought, they were master-craftsmen. Somehow they had accomplished the impossible, and that felt good.

CHAPTER 8

Black Wings of Mercy

Truck driver Wayne Tremblay would have gladly traded his driver's licence for a stiff drink that night as he
carefully edged the blunt-nosed truck away from Menzies Bay onto the Trans-Canada Highway and coaxed it
through a half-dozen gear changes. Every unusual noise
or the slightest load shift would cause him to search the
side-mounted rear-view mirrors for signs of an
emergency he hoped wouldn't happen. Like Davis,
Tremblay was surprised when the rescue crew simply
lashed the sling-encased whale onto the makeshift framing spiked to the expanse of the truck's after deck. He
had envisioned a sophisticated system of tanks and
hoses as the calf's overland stretcher.

What had really unnerved him was a five-minute
driving lecture by Wright.

"Your ability to drive fast but smoothly enough so that not one drop of water is lost out of those reservoir buckets is probably all that stands between life and death for this whale," Wright said, rolling a gnarled toothpick over his tongue and across his teeth.

"The stakes are loaded against you," he continued. "As you're probably aware there is only a one-in-a-thousand chance the calf is going to survive the trip. Your driving will either stabilize that chance or wipe it out entirely. Hyman and Matthews will be among five attendants riding on the back. They will give you speed up, slow down, and stop directions with a set of signals he will tell you about before you start."

The remainder of the terse monologue reviewed the location of water stops, alternate routes through several of the larger towns in the unlikely case of heavy traffic, and again stressed the importance of fast, smooth driving. Almost as an afterthought Wright wished him good luck.

Tremblay was another unwitting addition to the rescue team, shanghaied, so to speak, from behind the counter of the firm that had rented the truck to Sealand. As manager of the rental agency he had volunteered for the job and felt a twinge of excitement at the prospect. That sense of adventure had now faded into a palm-sweating battle of nerves that required the ultimate in driving skill. The highway that stretched before them had often lost cars and trucks to the gravel shoulders and thick forests that stretched alongside the hundreds of curves and sharp bends. And none of those ill-fated vehicles, including the eighteen-wheel semi-trailer freight trucks, had been forced to contend with the unstabilizing effects of a half-ton killer whale nervously flipping about in the back seat.

The drive had started with a bad omen, he thought as he wrestled the big four-spoke steering wheel and strained to see beyond the distance of the high-beam headlights. Before they had reached the highway Matthews had called for a stop underneath a massive wooden water tower similar to the reservoirs used in a bygone era to refuel water tanks of steam locomotives. This one, normally used to fill the brake-cooling systems of logging trucks, was being pressed into service to top up the whale ambulance water buckets. One of the rescue members who vowed a knowledge of such equipment tugged forcefully at a knotted cord that dangled above his head. Nothing happened. Not to be outdone by the device he jumped and dangled his weight from it. A split second later he was washed to the truck deck in a torrent of water that momentarily seemed to threaten a second world flood.

"I thought for sure the calf had been washed out to sea and was surprised to see it still firmly in the sling after the water had stopped," Matthews later said in recounting the incident. "If anything, though, it did the calf more good than harm. The tower soaked it more thoroughly than we ever could have by hand. And it did as much for the crew. We were as soaked as the whale but we didn't have the same need for cooling or the blubber to keep us warm. Even though it was a warm night, the wind hitting us on the open deck at highway speeds made us shiver convulsively for the entire trip. We didn't stop shivering for two hours after the trip. I was as cold then as I ever want to be and ironically it was in the middle of a heat wave, when a lot of people would have paid a month's wages to bathe in a bathtub full of ice cubes."

Although the wind chill began as soon as the truck

reached the highway, the crew put aside their own discomforts to attend the calf. As long as the truck was moving the baby whale stayed reasonably quiet, moving only enough from time to time to shift its weight in the oppressive gravity of the strange world outside the sea. The throaty growl of the engine, the whining hum of the thick-treaded truck wheels and the gusty blasts of wind, as well as the vehicle's movement, all seemed to comfort the calf. Perhaps the humid, womb-like interior of the sling further enhanced the baby's feeling of being protected. For both the calf and the crew the memories of the bay, with the shrill sound of outboard motors, the snorty growl of diesel engines and the squeals of pulleys, were washed into the afterwake of the truck to be absorbed by the star-prickled sky.

Although the Trans-Canada Highway, which lays north and south along the island's seemingly tame eastern seaboard, follows a relatively smooth coastline and escapes the mountainous regions inland, Matthews couldn't help but think the road had been designed by a survey crew that had maintained a love affair with a whiskey bottle. At any rate the crew had obviously lacked any knowledge of explosives or bridge construction, he mused, as the truck heaved first over one hill and rolled into the valley ahead, only to be met by another hill and a bent-elbow curve.

After leaving Menzies Bay the makeshift whale ambulance crept through the second- and third-growth fir trees that almost enclosed the road in a roofless tunnel as they made their slender reach for the sky. At Campbell River the truck broke into the eye-stabbing light of street lamps and neon store signs as it was guided along the seaward lay of the road on the northern outskirts of the town. It was here that the existence of land and

102

man-made things belied the true nature of the island's northern inside waters. The scrubby, waist-high trees and bushes had been grotesquely bent by unrelenting winds. Even the short, willowy grasses that grew where no tree or bush could get a life-grip, leaned protectively away from the onslaught of wind-lashed sea spray. And there were places where nothing grew – long flat stretches of rock-hard clay earth where the wind and sea had pummelled small craters into the naked ground.

Man-made oddities fared no better. The wharves – though there weren't many along the boulder- and log-strewn shoreline – were protected by log corrals and rubble heaps of rocks that formed breakwaters. Yet, even with this protection, there were remnants of storm-battered piers and twisted floating docks. On land the clutter of clapboard and stucco houses, as well as the box-square commercial buildings, visually reeked of their ongoing battle. As far as a quarter of a mile from the water, exterior window sills and ledges glistened under a coat of crystalline salt deposits flung from the ocean during the torment of a winter storm. In many places, painted surfaces had either cracked, peeled, or paled under the frequent punishment of the elements. Some people, armed with paint brushes and gallon cans, had sought to renew their home's defences annually while others had given up. In the cases of the latter the shore-side houses, many of them converted summer cottages, were weathered grey, showing only the smallest hint of ever having been painted.

However, the sea, with its system of checks and balances, had been as kindly to Campbell River as it had been tormenting. Out of the tidal depths came salmon, larger, more plentiful, and more accessible than anywhere on the Pacific Coast. Added to the logging and commercial fishing backbone of the town was the advent of a thriving sports-fishing business that attracted the continent's wealthiest men as well as movie stars, politicians, and the work-a-day men and women eager to hook into a big one. During the spring-summer salmon season, Campbell River has all the raucous gaiety of a gambling town. The parties and celebrations begin on the boats and, liquor-stimulated, continued in pubs, bars, and lounges, and later move into hotel rooms. That's not to say the town doesn't have its more serene and stable side of life, with well-painted houses and manicured yards, it's just not visible from the highway.

Matthews cast only a hurried glance at Fishermen's Wharf as they passed it and didn't really notice the covered barge near the road. Inside the bait barge Alec Hunt was beginning his early morning preparations for the expected crowd of sports fishermen who would be eager to buy bait and get to the fishing grounds before sun-up. Hunt didn't notice the truck as it rumbled past. Yet the two men, although never having met, would retain a bond through their concern over the whale calf.

Closer to the centre of the business area several loud parties were still moving full force into the early hours of Wednesday morning. The truck moved cautiously through light traffic and gave wide berth to a few straggling and swaying bottle-clutching fishermen. Despite shouts from a few people, and several horn honks from nearby cars, the calf remained quiet except for a short period when the truck was forced to stop at a traffic light. During the slow drive through the town Matthews scrambled onto the roof of the truck cab, leaned his head upside down through the driver's open side window and told Tremblay a water stop would be needed by the time they reached the next town.

The road was narrow and bumpy after it twisted inland out of Campbell River. It was a highway only by name. Although the jarring bumps in some sections rattled the truck from stem to stern it was a rougher ride for the crew than the whale. The iron poles which were lashed horizontally to the wooden framing built onto the truck, and from which the sling was suspended, absorbed most of the unexpected poundings of potholes and upheavals for the calf. But even at reduced speeds the twists, dives, and jolts of the old road forced the crew members to attend the calf with one hand clenching a post or railing. At the beginning of the journey, one of the rescuers was detailed to time the calf's breathing rate and to "sing out" if the rhythm varied more than a minute. Hyman continually talked to the baby and stroked its stiff and sore body while Matthews helped the other two crew members bail water onto the lanolin-smeared and cloth-covered whale form.

After driving past the farmlands at the northern edge of the Comox Valley, Tremblay stopped the truck at the first water stop – a brightly lit service station on the outskirts of Courtenay. The calf stayed quiet for a short while before it blew a spout and started vocalizing. It was just enough time for the crew to unload the empty buckets and ask about the location of the water hose.

"Have all the water you want," said the service station attendant, staring in the direction of the noise-filled, and breath-spouting sling.

"But would you mind telling me what it's for?"

"To wet down a killer whale," Matthews said without thinking about his answer.

"Look, fellah," the attendant persisted, "I've already told you that you can have all the water you want. If you don't want to tell me what it's for that's your business – it's free and there's no skin off my nose – but you don't have to get smart about it."

Matthews held up an open hand as if trying to ward off a fight.

"It's the truth. If you don't believe me climb onto the truck and take a look."

When the young service station attendant jumped back to the ground after a cautious peek into the sling he ignored the crew members, working to heave the full water containers back into place, and started talking to an unseen companion.

"They're nuts – really nuts. I can't tell anybody that I saw a killer whale a couple of miles from the ocean. You just don't tell people you had a killer whale pull up to the pumps for some water. I mean that sort of thing doesn't even happen at a marina fuel float. They're nuts – really nuts."

Matthews and Hyman laughed so hard they got stomach-aches. And the rest of the crew couldn't resist the humour of the situation after they realized just how strange the procession must look with Matthews and Hyman hugging each side of the deck in convulsive laughter while the whale blew steamy locomotive-type spouts that trailed back into the air while the truck was motored onto the highway. Even Tremblay laughed his way into third gear. In reality it was the laughter of exhaustion and an explosion of pent-up tension – the crew had worked more than thirty hours from the time of their departure from Victoria until now, with only an hour out the previous morning for a hurried nap. The service station attendant had done more than he ever knew to reunite the weary team and had caused the unit to revitalize its life-sustaining efforts toward the calf.

After the water stop the calf-bearing truck cruised

past the compact business section of Courtenay and stormed off in a snarl of gear changes toward the egress of Comox Valley. Having left the worst piece of road behind, Tremblay pushed the accelerator until the speedometer needle balanced delicately on the forty-five-mile-an-hour mark. Blink-and-you've-missed-them settlements, like the gas stop of Union Bay and the government licenced refreshment stop of Fanny Bay, were lost for the crew to the eye-watering wind caused by the truck's movement. The road, although narrow for being part of a national highway, was smooth with easy-flowing curves that followed the gentle undulations of the coastline. Tremblay pressed his advantage and the truck rumbled through the night at a daring fifty-five miles an hour. Not one car appeared on the road to hinder the progress of the mission and the calf nearly flew on its perch, as if the road had become the black wings of mercy.

The continuous, even-pitched hum of the wheels, and the rush of the wind, soothed the baby whale and its breathing rate remained steady at acceptable ninety-second intervals. But the apparent comfort of the calf didn't diminish the crew's activity or its concern. Matthews and Hyman were probably more aware than the others that the baby's life could be lost in the short time between breaths. Hyman knew the risks because he was a veterinarian, he had dealt with similar problems in dolphins and Beluga whales. Matthews had seen the morbid spectacle of a whale's death on several occasions: the last breath, drawn in the same sharp, concise way hundreds of previous breaths had been snatched from the atmosphere. Then, suddenly, there would be the realization that the whale was overdue for another breath. There would be the rush of divers and veterinarians, but before anyone could help, the death-relaxed muscles in the blowhole would part in a loud, blubbering exhaust and the whale would sink. This calf wouldn't sink – at least not for the moment – its perch on the deck of the truck ensured that. But both Matthews and Hyman knew that the secrets of the whale's physical and psychological system placed it an ocean apart from any man's understanding.

The endless task of pouring water onto the calf, soothing it with words and touches, and monitoring its breathing rate consumed all but a fraction of the crew's attention. They were barely conscious of their passage through the tourist-vacation villages of Qualicum Beach and Parksville. Hyman took advantage of the pallid light from the street lamps to make a hurried visual inspection of his patient while Matthews signalled Tremblay to make another water stop in Nanaimo, the next town on the map. Just north of Nanaimo – the largest city on the island with the exception of Victoria – the road finally revealed its identity as a part of the Trans-Canada Highway system by expanding into two wide lanes south and north. After having been forced by winding and hilly road conditions to restrict the truck's speed to forty miles an hour, Tremblay levelled his foot on the accelerator and shot the vehicle toward the centre of Nanaimo. The light traffic that circulated through the area was easily circumvented by using the passing lane that runs almost through the centre of the city.

Nanaimo looked grey as they entered it, even the vague sparkle of starlight did little to enhance its visual impact. It had none of the eye-catching adornments or splashes of colour that visitors look for in a city. For the most part the squat two- and three-storey business blocks were dirty looking except where a neon sign

108

rudely blurted out its message. Several men, workers in the nearby lumber mill, exchanged hearty patter outside one of the all-night cafés. Other men and women, some of them jean-jacketed native Indians, wandered aimlessly in and out of the shadows along the sidewalks.

Like most cities that exist on the periphery of a mill complex, Nanaimo has a vibrant, almost underground, nightlife. It is a life that is little known, and even if apparent, it is not accepted by the people who make up the city's daytime life. But Nanaimo has never been a city of superfluous trappings. It has always been a working town, built from an underground source – coal mining. The earth beneath the town is literally riddled with snaking mine shafts – some that extend well out below the sea bed of Nanaimo harbour. Some men got rich from these diggings but they weren't the ones who worked the dark, wet, and forbidding tunnels; those men got meagre wages and some succumbed to diseases for their efforts. Many of the coal barons had emigrated from Scotland and some returned to their homeland after making their fortunes. At least one Scottish baron fled to the picturesque sanctum of Victoria. It must have reminded him of home for there he built a massive stone castle that still exists.

The crew passed through the city without giving any thought to its subcultures or history-clad beginnings. The water buckets were empty and Matthews hoped Tremblay would soon find a service station. The only thing that trailed across his mind about the city – particularly the harbour – was that it was the first place that the calf had encountered friendly human beings. The calf, snuggled blindly in its sling, was not aware of its geographic location, but had it been, it would have certainly recalled its frantic flight from these grimy waters. In fact, had the calf been able to see and recognize any of the coastline they travelled along that night, it would have been able to recall a myriad of painful and frightening events.

It was 2:30 A.M. when the truck rolled to a stop for the second water refill of the journey. The service station varied little from the previous one. It was a different colour but the fuel pumps and water outlets were in the same position and the outdoor service area was lit by the same endless banks of fluorescent light tubes. Hyman was filling the last of the six buckets by the time the station attendant had walked unhurriedly to the water outlet. From the corner of his eye Hyman could see Matthews also walking towards him and thought both of them could use another laugh.

"You'll never guess what we need all this water for," he said as Matthews stopped beside them.

The attendant idly shrugged his shoulders and said, "I suppose it's for the killer whale that's coming down from being rescued up coast."

Hyman and Matthews looked at each other with naked surprise and then Matthews' face contorted into a frown.

Obviously the news media had finally gotten hold of the story, in this case the radio stations. There had been a reporter at the bay during part of the rescue, a girl from the weekly *Campbell River Courier*. But weekly news-papers are not usually part and parcel of the wire ser-vices that interconnect the flow of news between daily newspapers. Either there had been another reporter at the scene whom Matthews hadn't known about, or, possibly, the newspaper reporter had leaked her own front-page spread to a radio station. At any rate, if the wire services didn't have it now they soon would have.

Within a few hours the whole world would know about it. Matthews hoped they could make Victoria before too much publicity was stirred up – and he desperately hoped they arrived with a live whale. He looked at his watch and mentally pegged 4:30 A.M. as their arrival time in Victoria.

There were no towns directly between Nanaimo and Duncan, which gave the truck clear passage over more than fifty miles of freeway-style road. Tremblay had lost his nervousness gradually over the preceding hundred miles and replaced it with an all-consuming concern for the calf. He had forgotten about himself and, like the rest of the crew, had sucked one thought out of the breathless sky – every scrap of knowledge and trick of the trade had to be used to get that calf to Victoria, alive. Tremblay pushed the accelerator further than he had dared before. The fine needle of the speedometer buried itself in the numeral sixty. The truck crashed through the silence of the deserted highway and disappeared around well-banked curves in a glow of red tail lights.

Matthews felt channel fever mounting in him when they reached Duncan – the same fever that rose in British sailors when they reached the British Channel after long absences at sea. Victoria was forty-five miles away – an hour's drive – and it looked like they would make his estimated arrival time. There was just one major obstacle in the way now, the Malahat – a mountain that heaves the road up in a straight climb to 1,300 feet above sea level. The truck would make the climb, there was no question about that. He had just hoped the "Hat" didn't rob them of too much time by forcing the truck into the slow range of climbing gears. He needn't have worried.

Under the ham-fisted guidance of Tremblay the truck snarled into an attack of the mountain that threatened to rip it apart. Although the truck was forced into the lower range of gears, and Tremblay had to gear down the special rear axle, he made expert use of both the engine and gears, squeezing every ounce of power and speed they could give. If he lost any time going up he more than made up for it going down the other side. The altitude of the Malahat – infamous for causing temporary ear blockages in people – affected the calf's breathing so that it blew every fifteen seconds. Halfway down the mountain the calf seemed to regain its breath and in so doing put to rest the worst fears of the anxious crew.

At the southern foot of the mountain the truck wound through the cool, moist forest that overhangs the road along the Goldstream river, and then it climbed out of the shallow valley to make the final run to Victoria. The highway entrance to the outskirts of British Columbia's capital city is like the entrance to a thousand other middle-sized cities. If it has any distinguishing aspects it is probably that it looks a little disorganized, a little cluttered. The main street route that the truck followed toward the centre of town afforded few of the embellishments and little of the character the tourist brochures repute the city to have. Much of the character is centred around the city's harbour and the truck left the main thoroughfare, heading toward the suburb municipality of Oak Bay, long before it neared the tourist attractions.

On the outskirts of Oak Bay Matthews signalled Tremblay to stop at a cleanly-painted bungalow of indeterminable age. It was one of two sister houses, squatting side by side, that Matthews owned. He occupied the one closest to the truck and said it would be a good place to refill the depleted water reserves. Although it was less than two miles to the pool that had been chosen as the calf's recovery site, it was expected the transfer would take at least another half-hour and the calf would still require wetting during that time.

Tremblay left the truck engine idling as he helped fill and carry the buckets. The water for the last reservoir had just been drawn, and the container secured aboard the truck, when the engine sputtered to a stop. Tremblay shrugged and jumped back into the cab while the crew restationed themselves on the back deck. He confidently twisted the ignition key between his thumb and forefinger. Nothing happened. He tried a second time, slamming it harder into the start position. Still nothing happened. A third try got the same response. He called out the side window for Matthews.

"A dead battery," Matthews shouted after hearing Tremblay's report.

But the anguish had little time to settle before he had assembled the crew in front of the truck to push it backwards down the street. The effort, he hoped, would serve to jump-start the vehicle and he prayed the battery still had enough juice to fire the engine. They pushed it backwards because the road inclined slightly downhill in that direction, despite the fact that it was the wrong way down a one-way street. It was 4:30 A.M., the night was moving into dawn. Even in the dim light any cars that happened along could see the bulk of the truck and steer around it, Matthews thought. The lights had been switched off to conserve what little energy the battery might still have had.

Matthews wasn't quite sure at that point whether it was luck or misfortune that made the first and only car along the road a black and white Victoria Police patrol unit. He told the crew to keep pushing no matter what happened. The constable was a little disconcerted at first to be forced to trot along beside this obvious moving violation. But after a panted explanation by Matthews and a quick glance into the sling he pocketed his ticket book and added his muscle to the grunting crew who were heaving themselves into the front of the truck. The men kept pushing vigorously as the truck gathered speed down the slight incline, and finally, more than 300 yards from where the engine had stopped, Tremblay eased the clutch out. The engine sputtered and coughed once before it rumbled to life.

Later that morning the constable struggled to type a report of the incident. He filled a waste-paper basket to overflowing with crumpled and discarded versions before simply writing, "4:40 A.M., assisted in restarting whale-carrying truck." "If nothing else it will give the filing clerks something to talk about during coffee break," he mused. "Might even get me a couple of extra weeks' leave on doctor's orders." He chuckled at the thought as he pigeon-holed the report at the charge desk and signed off shift.

At Sealand, Matthews had Tremblay park the truck beside the only car in the parking lot. He reached into the unlocked Mercedes Benz and pulled the hood release. A couple of minutes later he had switched the dead truck battery for the fully-charged car battery and the truck was headed the last half-mile to the Oak Bay Beach Hotel.

"Wright never knew his battery was missing until we asked him later if we could put it back in," Matthews laughingly recalled.

Matthews later termed the calf's arrival at the hotel pool as "organized pandemonium."

"It was an onslaught of people and equipment. Everyone was asking questions – is the calf still alive?

how did it fare the trip? were there any bad moments?

"At the same time, a bunch of guys – some that I'd never seen before – were laying sheets of plywood in a row down the lawn urging Tremblay to back the truck over them. As the truck backed over one piece a couple of people would grab it and reposition it at the far end of the wooden roadbed. A medium-sized crane that was beside the pool had obviously been coaxed across the lawn in the same manner."

Matthews and Hyman remained on the back of the truck to soothe the calf and keep it wetted down. Hoey had joined them as soon as the truck had pulled into the parking lot. It was half an hour before the flatdeck was jostled in beside the crane and another half-hour before the sling was connected and balanced on the end of the crane cable. It was during the period of sling adjustments that Hoey and Hyman were able to get their first close look at the calf's underside.

"It's a girl!" Hyman shouted.

At 6:30 A.M., an hour after arriving at the pool, the calf made a gentle splashdown into the enclosure amid cheers and a dozen pairs of helping hands. Hyman watched anxiously as the whale slowly swam away from the submerged sling and pulled her first breath in the pool.

"She's a miracle," he said, breaking the silence that had fallen while she was lowered into the pool. "A one-in-a-thousand chance of surviving the trip and she grabbed it."

"Miracle. That will be her name," Wright said quietly. He turned his eyes away from the calf and looked out to sea past the nearby islands to the sun-painted waters of Juan de Fuca Strait. Only a slight rasp in his voice had betrayed his emotions.

116

CHAPTER 9

Death Stalks a Baby

The rescue team was afforded little time for self-congratulations or a much needed rest. The bouncing trip along the twisting Trans-Canada Highway had exacted a greater toll on Miracle than showed outwardly. The five-hour trip had actually been an extremely traumatic experience for the ailing calf. Minutes after being placed in the recovery pool she went into shock. Spasms shook her fragile frame and she vocalized convulsively.

Selected members of the rescue team jumped into the partially filled pool with the whale calf, rubbing and trying to soothe her out of the shock. Badly needed blood tests – the only reasonably accurate way to determine the intensity of the calf's wounds, under the

117

circumstances – would have to wait until the shock sub-sided. There was nothing anyone could do but wait and let the whale know that her friends were close by. Anything more than that was up to Miracle.

Within half an hour the shock did diminish and several of the rescue team members who had remained in the pool climbed out of the enclosure for a rest and food. Only Hyman remained in the water and he did so more out of a reaction to a vague veterinary inclination than for any specific reason. At the edge of the pool Hoey was readying instruments for a blood test while Wright circled the pool side in a moment of quiet, which had become rare during the last two days. The veterinarians were talking quietly over the short distance between them, discussing the best place on the scarred whale from which to draw a blood sample – Hoey was also rummaging through the dark confines of his medical bag for viles to contain the samples – when a panicky shout decreed impending disaster.

"She's down," Wright yelled as he splashed into the pool. "For God's sake help her – she's sunk."

"There's bubbles," someone else shouted.

Hyman was already reaching into the shallow water, trying desperately to raise the calf to the surface. Even before Wright had reached the submerged calf, bubbles had begun to burst to the surface from the baby's blowhole – the final marker of a whale's death.

Shortly before she sunk Miracle made a plea for help. She had been swimming slowly counter-clockwise when she suddenly aborted the circle to swim directly towards Hyman. Ten feet away from the veterinarian Miracle doubled up, as if she had been seized by a crippling cramp, and managed a short, broken cry before she sunk. Medical bags and partially eaten plates of food were thrown to the ground as the rescue team rushed into the pool to help raise the 850-pound whale to the surface again.

The pool was still being filled and at this point the water level, even at the deep end, was less than three and a half feet. Yet even in the sure footing of the shallow depths, and within the neutral buoyancy of the salt water, it was difficult for the team to hold Miracle's limp body at the surface. As the crew struggled to keep the calf afloat and carry her to the shallow end where she could be laid above water on a foam-rubber pad stretched across the rocks, Hoey intermittently jammed one of his knees into Miracle's chest. He knew that heart massage was impossible; there was no way that human hands could manipulate through even Miracle's skimpy layer of blubber and penetrate the heavy rib structure that guarded her heart cavity. His only hope was that the blows would vibrate the heart enough to restart it. It was a very desperate chance and would work only if Miracle still maintained her will to live, and if there was still a spark of electricity in her body to motivate the life rhythms of the life-giving organ.

A blind man would have been as touched by the struggles of the crew as a sighted person. The pool, which moments earlier had been quiet except for the methodical breaths of the whale, was now a cacophony of shouted instructions pierced by pleadings to the whale to give life signs. But the harshest sound was the silence created by the absence of the whale's exhaling breath, exploding raggedly into the morning air followed instantly by the sharp suck of a fresh breath. Yet, any man would have felt his stomach turn at the primeval stench that silently escaped the calf's blowhole in the final exhaust of death.

Hyman shouted for someone to bring him a stethoscope, though not one word had been traded between the veterinarians who continued to grapple feverishly with the fading chance of the whale's revival. Miracle's stillness betrayed her condition before Hyman's anguished report that "her heart has stopped" was launched into the air like a poison cloud. While Hoey flung himself to the edge of the pool in search of his medical bag Hyman and the other team members continued pummelling Miracle's body in hopes of restarting her heart. For a while – long minutes stretched from agonizing seconds – nothing happened. Hoey returned in a splashing gait across the shallow end of the pool to plunge a four-inch-long syringe into the whale's back beside the dorsal fin. Still nothing happened. He unloaded a second syringe full of steroids – a stimulant used to strengthen metabolic rates – into the same area. For more tense seconds the baby remained motionless, lost to the secret, final world of death. And then her body tensed, sending nervous ripples along the length of her rubbery body. The ripples increased until they became spasmodic waves of shivers and then she sucked a shallow but sharp breath of air. Miracle had technically died at 7:30 A.M., two hours after arriving at the hotel pool. Fifteen minutes later she was alive again, her life-hungry breaths rebounding their sound off the pool walls. But no one could ensure that the baby's revival was anything more than a respite from a final death that could lay minutes or months into the future. For Hoey the calf's death and her revival drove home a number of realizations.

"We weren't dealing with a normal killer whale. Even without all the facts that we were able to gather later, I knew then that Miracle should have never lived long

enough to harbour herself in Menzies Bay; that even though she did land in the bay and lived on sheer will power, it was almost medically impossible for her to have survived the overland trip to Victoria. Miracle's revival from death was the first time that man took any significant part in her struggle. It was her will power and our limited knowledge. In effect Miracle had said, 'I can't carry on the fight alone anymore, I need help.' I prayed that we could uphold our end."

Miracle's revival also ended Hoey's self-made promise to remain clinical and objective about the calf's struggle for survival. That one crisis plunged him into an emotional involvement with Miracle that rivalled Davis's love of the whale. Sleepless nights spent pacing the floors of his apartment were, for the veterinarian, anxieties of a medical nature. The long, dark hours so spent contained the worries of procedure and of drug dosages; it was the pensive mind-search for clues – any clues – of the internal enemies that threatened the baby. And later in the battle for the whale's life, the pacing accompanied the recall of blood test results and the desperate search for one significant, possibly minute, detail in the report that would pinpoint Miracle's gravest ailment. But more often, Hoey would visit the pool. Sometimes he would pace and sometimes he would just sit and marvel at this baby queen of the oceans. On these occasions all observations, and any diagnosis that might evolve, were shrouded in emotion.

Even after Miracle was revived, and the rescue team had launched her back into the pool to keep her from being dried out by the sun, she had to be walked around the pool for twenty minutes before she could swim without sinking. The method involved each member of the rescue team taking turns supporting the whale at the surface and slowly carrying her through the water. Later that first day, Hoey and Hyman tried three times before they were successfully able to take a blood sample. Under analysis the blood showed the white cell count to be 9,500 – well above what was believed to be a normal count of 6,000. (It was later learned that a count of 7,000 was actually closer to normal for a baby killer whale.) However, the analysis did prove what the veterinarians had suspected earlier, that Miracle was fighting an exceedingly high level of infection.

The next day, Thursday, August 11, Miracle sank to the bottom of the pool three times. Although her heart continued to beat through all the emergencies this time, she would have drowned had the medical-rescue team not hauled her back to the surface. The truth was that Miracle was exhausted – so exhausted that she couldn't keep herself buoyant. She was placed on forced rest, a system that allowed her to swim under supervision for fifty minutes before being placed on the padded rocks for a ten-minute rest.

That night Wright called the first of ten marathon-style meetings which would punctuate a variety of crises throughout the next three months. The meetings, involving Sealand managerial staff, the veterinarians, and any outside experts that could be found, were never less than five hours in length and were always stormy. Wright worked on two theories during these meetings – or sessions, as they were not-so-fondly called by the participants. A person would never fully communicate his ideas unless forced into a heated argument, and a proper decision could never be made until all negative and positive arguments had been aired. Hoey was grateful for Wright's tactless and persistent approach to the calf's ailments.

"His hard-nosed attacks brought a quality to veterinary medicine that is rarely seen in the profession. He not only wanted answers but all sides of the problem as well. If there were five different ways to approach a particular crisis he wanted to know why a particular avenue was taken or why it was in the process of being chosen. He wanted to know all the ins and outs of the other four possibilities. Hyman and myself were able to bounce theories off one another and to use each other's past experiences. Often we would leave a lot unsaid because we understood medicine. When we went up against Wright nothing was left unsaid or untouched. He not only forced communication, he forced us to rethink the problems and the diagnosis. He, in effect, was a proving-ground for decisions."

Friday was the first "normal" day for Miracle and the people who guarded her recovery, but still nothing was being left to chance. Three eight-hour shifts comprising four people on each watch, stood guard over the whale calf day and night. As an added safety precaution Hyman's hotel room was located so that it looked out directly over the recovery pool. When he wasn't personally tending the calf he posted standing instructions to call him if the slightest abnormal behaviour occurred.

On Saturday, after more blood analysis, Miracle was taken off the critical list and her apparent overnight recovery released her from forced rest periods. An even more encouraging sign was that she now accepted sole fillets as an addition to her vitamin-enriched herring diet. At night the medical-rescue crew recorded improved sleeping patterns in the whale calf, although at one point they over-reacted and woke her because they thought she was in trouble. At another time they prodded her to wakefulness purposely to check the length of time it took for her to regain sleep. The verdict, two minutes, certainly did not indicate insomnia under the circumstances.

There was little wonder that Miracle slept well that night. Aside from being serenaded by internationally recognized flautist, Paul Horn, the calf had been reunited with Davis – an event that had deep emotional impact on both whale and man. Matthews was alternately amused and awed by the reactions to Davis's visit.

"Nobody remembered what Davis looked like, including me, so I got one of the team members to check his driver's licence. We were keeping pretty tight security on the calf at that point. While Davis started rummaging through his wallet for the identification Miracle started acting strange – going crazy. She was heaving herself in and out of the water and speed swimming toward the wall, missing it each time by inches. We thought she was going to have an attack of some kind, or at the very least she was going to injure herself on the cement pool walls. When Davis, who was still standing on the spectator side of the fence, suggested that Miracle recognized his voice we laughed. But it wasn't long before we were believers. When Miracle saw Davis approaching the side of the pool she broke loose from the three men trying to restrain her and shot directly toward him."

Miracle's speed and stop-action manoeuvre was such that the waves that hit the edge of the pool were splashed skyward in a plume that drenched Davis. He was bending over the pool when the calf spontaneously propelled her body halfway out of the water to meet him in a chin-nuzzling hug that knocked his sun-glasses into the water. Davis made no effort to hide his tears. Later that day the two of them lunched together after Davis climbed into the pool with a bucket of herring for the calf. As well as the sun-glasses that had been retrieved from the bottom of the pool Davis wore a special shirt with the inscription "Miracle, Campbell River" blazoned in two rows across the front.

The first crowds of visitors began gathering around the pool that weekend and the commotion seemed to be to the calf's liking. On Sunday the blood test showed a decrease in white cell production – a sign that the killing infection was being beaten. Her strength had also increased; she continually swam around the pool, playfully knocking over attendants whenever she could. And she was eating more. But the celebrations of her recovery lived only a few hours into the night. Shortly after dark she sank to the bottom of the pool again, although the duty team wasn't able to discern whether it was caused by a medical disorder or whether it was a natural behavioural trait.

The whale calf was closely monitored and kept quiet throughout the day Monday. Further blood tests continued to show a decrease in the white cell production. By the end of the uneventful day both Hoey and Hyman were convinced that Miracle was on the mend and they were sure that the one thing she needed more than anything was rest. With that diagnosis sufficiently proven to Wright the veterinarians were able to bargain for their first night off, which they put to use by attending a lacrosse game in Victoria. The game had been in progress less than two minutes inside the capital city's Memorial Arena and the home team Shamrocks had already scored a goal against the visiting mainland team when the public address system rattled out an urgent message.

"Sealand veterinarians Dr. Jay Hyman and Dr. Alan

Hoey, report to the main office for an emergency message."

A game official called for time in the middle of play as the veterinarians hurdled over the empty seats in front of them, jumped the wooden barrier onto the playing surface and sprinted along the edge of the court. Having gained the main office and received the message that Miracle had again sunk to the bottom of the pool, the men pushed through a nearby exit and ran a block and a half to Hoey's car. Hoey slowed for a number of red traffic lights that blocked his path but he didn't stop. He was unaware that he was being followed. Along the relatively straight stretches of road he accelerated the car up to fifty miles an hour, horn-honking his way past slower, law-abiding motorists. Hyman said later that he saw very little scenery during the drive, except for what little he could visually capture during the split-second glimpses he dared to take over the passenger's dashboard. For the most part, though, he remembers having his body rolled up tightly and stashed safely at the bottom of the seat.

Hoey's swift entrance into the hotel parking lot threatened to send his vehicle sailing over the embankment to join Miracle at the bottom of the pool. At the last moment he employed both the foot and emergency hand brakes to stop the car at the end of a fifty-foot-long set of smoking skid marks that were etched into the pavement. As the two men began to run across the parking lot toward the pool Hoey recognized three men who were in close pursuit. Even on the gallop he identified them as two reporters and a photographer from the daily newspapers. Later he learned that the media men had been covering the game when the emergency call had been announced. Any hopes they had of covering the big story – Miracle's death – evaporated when they reached poolside. Miracle was swimming complacently around the pool amid a group of bewildered rescuers. Apparently she had not sunk but merely laid on the bottom of her own conscious and free will. She had surfaced moments after the duty team had placed the emergency call. Nevertheless Hyman said he would stay with the baby while Hoey retrieved Hyman's wife and his own girl friend from the game.

As a matter of courtesy Hoey stopped at the arena's main office to report Miracle's satisfactory condition. A few minutes later, as he squeezed down the aisle of seats towards the ladies he was to escort home, the announcer cut into play to publicly repeat the report. The news was given cheers and applause, louder and longer than that brought on by any goal that night, despite the home team's sixteen-point victory over the visiting players.

Miracle's health, though generally improving, remained in a fluctuating state for several days. At one point her food intake – another reasonably accurate method of monitoring a whale's health – was down, but at the same time the all-important white cell count had diminished to a safe level. All things taken into consideration Miracle was showing signs of an amazingly fast recovery. There was just one newly developed habit that was concerning the medical-rescue team: the whale calf swam with her jaws open. She looked ferocious in this new performance though she changed nothing in her gentle behaviour.

On August 9, the veterinarians made a detailed study of the calf's mouth. Their findings made history in killer whale research. Miracle was teething. Two baby teeth were cutting through the gums at the front of the lower jaw. They were the last of the whale's awesome mouthful of teeth to develop. The significance of the find was that, until the discovery of Miracle's new teeth, experts believed killer whales were born with a full set of forty or fifty conically shaped teeth. Scientists have since theorized that the two lower front teeth must develop later to allow the whale calves easier nursing. Not to mention the wear and tear saved on the mother.

Miracle improved daily over the next week, enabling the veterinarians to concentrate on some of her more minor problems. Although her skin was also continuing to improve and the wounds healing, there was concern about surface infections along her belly and right side. Some more prodding by medical teams produced another history-making find, although of lesser importance. Miracle was suffering from acne, probably due to her poor diet in the wild. Acne, common at certain periods of growth in humans, has also been known to appear in land animals, but Miracle's case was the first reported in ocean dwelling mammals.

The days continued their rush toward the end of summer in a maze of medical analysis and ensuing treatments. One day – or for several days – Miracle would be riding high on the road to recovery only to be plunged the next day into the abyss of near death. During particularly bad stretches the highs and lows occurred within hours of each other. Such was the day of Thursday, August 25. It was a confusing day, to say the least, for those close to the whale calf. Following an extensive physical examination that morning, Miracle was given her first clean bill of health, only to have it repealed later in the day. A second physical in the afternoon, coupled with Miracle's refusal to eat, led to a diagnosis of bleeding ulcers. Although the bleeding stopped later the same day, as suddenly and mysteriously as it had begun, it wasn't to be the end of the problem.

Miracle's condition seemed to remain stable until Sunday when she was again ravaged by internal bleeding. This time the veterinarians weren't sure what was causing the condition but they were beginning to realize that a hasty diagnosis was often as bad as no diagnosis. After seeking the opinions of marine mammal experts in the nearby cities of Vancouver and Seattle, Hoey contacted veterinarians in Guelph, Ontario, and in San Diego, California, and then asked the advice of blood experts at the University of Pennsylvania. When all the advice and opinions had been gathered and analyzed, Hoey and Hyman theorized that the internal bleeding could be the result of an ulcer, but also conceded the problem could be caused by parasites or undetected damage from the gunshot wound. In keeping with the latter possibilities Miracle's antibiotic drug intake was stepped up and, on Monday, the partially healed bullet wound was probed.

On Tuesday the calf threw another curve at the perplexed veterinarians – her white blood cell count was analyzed as being near normal, and her food intake had almost doubled to forty-two pounds daily, up from a low of twenty-four pounds. And again the veterinarians, cautiously and with guarded optimism, reduced the calf's heavy daily dosage of antibiotics.

The next ten days were uneventful, even though the routine practice of needle-poking medicals continued. That's not to say the baby whale wasn't bothered by recurrences of internal bleeding, but the fluctuating condition didn't seem to bother her overall health. It was only a brief respite in the see-saw battle for the calf's life.

On Sunday, September 11, she missed a mid-afternoon feeding – an event noteworthy for Sealand staff. The next morning, after another session with Wright, the veterinarians started a treatment for ulcers, which meant smaller amounts of food more often for the ailing calf. She refused two feedings that day. Concerned that ulcers might be only one of three things causing the loss of appetite – the other two being a common stomach-ache or a stomach blockage – the veterinarians also started giving Miracle an agent to soften the contents of the stomach. Red dye tests, designed to show up an intestinal blockage, were also started. Again Miracle regained her appetite but an irregular swimming pattern seemed to further indicate a stomach blockage. For the second time in three days the calf was taken off food.

Hoey and Hyman were totally caught up in the pendulum swings of Miracle's recoveries and regressions. They savoured each victory – no matter how small – yet they were aware that the winning of a battle could be within a finger-snatch of losing the war. In effect both could occur simultaneously. There was still a life-threatening churning taking place in the depths of Miracle's body and both veterinarians knew that the curtailment of the calf's food was robbing her of much needed nutrition. They also knew that to feed her when she couldn't digest the food was tantamount to poisoning her. So they were caught in an impossible situation with only the hope that time would prove to be an ally.

The veterinarians were so involved with the complications of the life battle that they gave little attention to the world that existed outside the fenced confines of Miracle's pool. Yet there was one event shaping up on the outside that the veterinarians wouldn't be able to ignore – it would be the first external threat to the whale calf's life since the event of her gunshot wound.

CHAPTER 10

Dr. Doolittle and the Flim Flam Man

Miracle took Victoria by surprise. Her gutsy fight for life against all odds caused the city to rally to her support and, for a short time, allowed many people to flee their own problems. Some of those problems were personal in nature while others stemmed from unsettled conditions across the country and throughout the world – the brewing threat of the Province of Quebec's separation from the rest of the country and unemployment figures that rivalled those produced during the depression years of the 1930s. Further uncertainty of the times was fuelled by the decreasing value of the Canadian dollar on foreign money markets.

Victorians found that they couldn't hide behind the façade of well-trimmed gardens and old English charm – that their city also harboured the ranks of the unemployed. In fact, Victoria topped the list several times when province by province head counts of the unemployed were made. Yet, at the same time, the British Columbia capital boasted its share of the wealthy – the people who were not generally touched by the fluctuations of the market place and who had little appreciation of the struggles of the unemployed. But for several months Miracle touched the heart of the city and brought together the rich, not so rich, and the poor.

A stack of get well cards for Miracle were stamped ornately with the return addresses of the Uplands – Victoria's highest-class residential area – while other return addresses marked the working-class areas of James Bay, Victoria West, and the middle-class suburb of Gordon Head. Few seemed untouched by Miracle's fight for life. Letters of sympathy and other penned inscriptions contained words of hope and prayer from the United States and far flung countries of Europe. During the first weeks, the local newspapers, and western Canada's largest news disseminating machine, *The Vancouver Sun,* ran the rescue stories on the front page underneath large black headlines. And for the first three months no Miracle story was ever placed further back than the front page of the second section.

While the avalanche of get well cards delivered to both the Oak Bay Beach Hotel and Sealand forced special mail deliveries, Matthews and Wright were faced with another dilemma. Cash donations, some tucked between the folds of get well cards, others stuffed anonymously in envelopes and dropped into the mail, and others hand delivered, posed a question of ethics. Sealand was not by any means a non-profit organization but suddenly they found themselves in the receipt of free money. After a hurried meeting with the company lawyer Matthews earmarked the donations as a food fund for the whale. The idea caught fire in a community eager to help and it infected tourists as well as residents. Those who couldn't afford cash donations, or wanted to make more specific gifts to the whale, offered fresh salmon, often the bounty of a sports fishing trip. Many others crowded around the spectator fence in an effort to lend moral support.

During August, September, and part of October, Miracle's supporters grew to a daily crowd of 3,000. Although many out-of-towners lined up to get a glimpse of the miracle whale, the bulk of onlookers were residents, and many of that group made daily pilgrimages to the site. At one point early in her recovery struggle Miracle was made an official part of a wedding reception which was held on the hotel lawn. In a few short weeks the baby whale had become the focal point of the coast. Radio stations made hourly broadcasts about her health during the crises of the early weeks and later broke into scheduled programing to report the latest threat to the plucky whale.

Not everyone shared in the enthusiasm of Miracle's rescue, however. Under the cover of dusk one evening, during the calf's second week at the hotel pool, a shabby relic of what was once a sixty-foot pleasure boat, hauled up short of the reefs outside the pool and dropped anchor. It was sun-up the next day before the burgee, snapping restlessly at the head of the boat's short cabin-top mast, could be identified as the insignia of the Greenpeace organization. Sealand and Greenpeace had often been at loggerheads over whale issues and, upon seeing the flag, Matthews braced his crew for an onslaught of abuse and criticism.

Throughout the day the boat nodded to the ebb and flow of tides, but little life was in evidence aboard the craft. None of the crew made any effort to go ashore. Finally, Matthews traced his eye along the decks of the boat with the aid of a pair of binoculars. His efforts revealed that he was also being watched. A half-dozen pairs of binoculars, prefacing a row of capped heads, were staring back at him in a line atop the high bulwarks of the vessel. It was the only contact Matthews was to have with the organization. That night, following the rumble and clatter of anchor chain being piled on the deck, the boat churned across the bay and disappeared behind a pair of nearby islands.

Greenpeace never publicly acknowledged Miracle through their own organization. A Victoria newspaper reporter, who contacted the Vancouver office of Greenpeace to get a reaction to the rescue, was told to go away, but in terms that were not as polite. Greenpeace did, however, add shadow support to another group that thought the time right for their appearance. That group did manage to wrestle away some of Miracle's limelight – even if they did find the attention was short and sour.

The group – actually a twosome comprising Stanley Burke, publisher of a mid-Vancouver Island weekly newspaper, and Bruce Bott, a former Sealand employee – announced a daring and somewhat expensive plan to send the calf back into the wild. It was instantaneously dubbed the Free Miracle Campaign and just as quickly got shot down in a blaze of flames by the press and denounced by the public. Timing was not one of the duo's fortes. They announced the plan at a press conference in late August, during a week when the calf's recuperation had taken a turn for the worse. The

scheme infuriated Wright, who had empowered Sealand to spend the more than $1,000 daily it was taking
to keep the baby alive.

"Whatever happens to Miracle," Wright shouted at a
reporter, "she will never be permitted to go to a bush
league Dr. Doolittle and his Flim Flam Man."

Burke, who was supposed to drum up public sympathy for the plan and gain the $25,000-worth of dona-
tions, which he said were needed for the program, was
of course the Flim Flam Man. Bott was blessed as Dr.
Doolittle because of his amazing ability to persuade the
government in a previous year to finance a summer of
drifting around Johnstone Straight in an effort to communicate with the whales. There were several reports,
though, that claimed he not only failed to communicate
with the mammals but actually failed to sight any.

Although Bott generously declined any payment for
his involvement in the scheme he did admit that part of
the $25,000 would be used for the rental of his
boat – the same boat that the government had bought
for the so-called Johnstone Strait studies, and later
gifted to him in total for all time. And with a futuristic eye
towards the calf's release Bott said part of the public
donation would be used to equip members of his group
with some type of mechanical assistance that would
allow them to swim as fast as the whale. (Killer whales
have been clocked at speeds in excess of thirty miles an
hour and it is not known whether or not that is their top
speed.) The remainder of the money would be used, he
said, to purchase filming equipment to record the
release.

Wright was not the only person angered by the
scheme. Victoria, and particularly Oak Bay, is noted for
an abundance of spritely little old ladies who look de-

ceivingly as fragile as wounded hummingbirds, but who champion a variety of causes as viciously and tenaciously as incensed bull dogs. One such lady was a thrice-daily visitor to Miracle's pool. Her punctuality could put computer-clocks to a test. Her first visit would be promptly at 10:00 in the morning, the next at 2:00 in the afternoon, and a final "look-see" of the day in the evening at 7:00 sharp. During each visit she would wave a lacy white handkerchief in Miracle's direction and unabashedly bawl out the calf's name in tones that made the attending crew wince with pain. Aside from her ear-assaulting yell, she was a kindly old woman who often "chatted-up" any spectators on either side of her. Kindly that was until someone unsuspectingly stepped upon her beliefs and then, with the courage of the old country, and the set jaw of Winston Churchill, she would set out to do battle.

The newest recruit of the Free Miracle Campaign was young, earnest, naïve, and indeed unsuspecting when he asked the old lady if she too wanted "a piece of the action" in exchange for a contribution of whatever she might be able to afford. She gave him a piece of the action by donating the working end of her walking cane to his buttocks. Ultimately stunned by this reception the lad found his feet unwilling to move and he watched helplessly as three more whacks were delivered to his backside. Finally he convinced his legs to flee but only to find the manic woman in hot pursuit. Not being able to successfully reach the lad's buttocks as he strove to push his way out of the crowd, the lady brandished the cane around his head and shoulders, hurling obscenities that would have been the pride of many a logger.

The old lady's action reflected the collective view of Victorians and the whale freeing scheme receded with a whimper, the last of which appeared in Burke's personal newspaper columns. Several federal fisheries people, now convinced that the whale should be given all the medical attention possible, told Wright they would oppose any move to place the whale back into the wild at any time, but especially in her current condition. Michael Bigg and the veterinarians echoed the response. Both Hoey and Hyman said the whale was incapable of dealing with any further external pressures – their report noted that the prolonged shock that would accompany Miracle's release into the wild would be as lethally threatening as the infected bullet wound. Bigg drew on his team's eight years of study to report the calf would never be able to survive in the wild because she had obviously never learned how to hunt – a skill that has to be taught to killer whales, passed down from generation to generation. Right or wrong Miracle's lot was to be with man – if she lived.

Emotions were no less charged inside the wire fence around the pool than they were outside. Hoey referred to the crisis periods – the alternating good and bad days – as "a time of yo-yo spirits."

"It was tough. It sucked the energy right out of us but we always managed to find some more power – a second, a fifteenth, a thirtieth wind. One day you would be up and the next day your butt would be driven ten feet into the ground. The worst part was knowing that the whale depended on you – for that matter anybody who'd ever heard of Miracle was depending on us to make a cure. People wanted solid answers. We did too, but we couldn't find any. One day a blood analysis would indicate a particular problem and the next day there would be no indication whatsoever that there was a problem. On the third day something completely different would show up in the blood samples."

Davis was kept thoroughly informed of the calf's progress, or as it often happened, her regress. He was phoned twice daily by Matthews and given a full medical report as well as an explanation in layman's language of just what the report meant in terms of survival. On Miracle's good days Davis felt immensely happy, secure in the knowledge that he had played a large part in saving the infant whale's life. On the bad days he was remorseful and almost angry that he was part of an operation that was succeeding only in prolonging the calf's suffering.

Neither was Wright left unscathed by the highs and lows of Miracle's struggle. He wore his thinly disguised feelings on his shirt sleeve – really believing they didn't show. His bewilderment and exasperation surfaced in anger, an anger that also had its base in a feeling of helplessness. He was rarely able to confine the feelings of anguish – to hide them silently in the pit of his chest as Davis did – instead he released them in verbal torrents. More often than not Matthews and the veterinarians took the brunt of the verbal flailings and sometimes they were unleashed onto the lower echelons of the medical-rescue teams. Some of the members had been unable to cope with the assaults and they had fallen from the ranks long before the advent of Miracle's rescue. The stout, dedicated group that remained either understood Wright's emotional composition or had the ability to fend off the abuse like so much water off a duck's back.

During mid-August, at a time when one unexplainable crisis after another threatened to snuff out the whale's life, Wright would often take advantage of a sleepless night to visit Miracle. For the most part he was

quiet and withdrawn during the sojourns, which consumed one to three hours of the early morning. He would sit at the edge of the pool, saying little to the graveyard shift crew, content to watch the calf drift through the water in the slow undulations of sleep.

One night the crew had been at their stations a little less than two hours when Wright told them to take a break to grab a cup of coffee from the drip-o-lator that had been left for their use in the hotel lobby. He waited until the crew had disappeared into the back door of the hotel before he took up a position at the edge of the pool. He watched the near-still form of the whale for several long minutes and then broke the silence in a low, muffled tone.

"I've never known an animal with your stubbornness – it's the one thing that's kept you alive. If you could only talk . . . but you can't, at least not in any language I can understand. God, I wish I had all the answers to heal you."

The baby woke with a start that made her tail flukes shudder. She blew and sucked a breath before sighting Wright and then slowly moved over to him. He pulled off his shoes and socks and then carefully draped his feet over the edge of the pool until he could rub the whale's back with the soles of his bare feet. The baby vocalized her approval and rolled over to have her stomach rubbed. While enjoying the feeling of the whale's cold, rubbery skin on his feet, Wright's mind flitted to the ambiguous results of the blood tests.

"I guess we're destined to help each other, Miracle. I make your back and stomach feel good and you do wonders for a pair of aching feet. I know you're trying to help us. Those blood results should tell us everything we need to know, if only we could find the clues. I say a lot of ifs and onlys, don't I? But you just hang in there with everything you've got because you and I and the others are going to change the only ifs – "

A soft sound and a shadow glimpsed from the corner of his eye caused Wright to drop the remainder of the sentence. It was one of the on-duty crew members who had come back with an offering of coffee.

"Have you been there long?" Wright asked.

"A minute or so," came the unsteady reply.

"So now you know that I talk to whales and rub them with my bare feet at 2:00 in the morning. Maybe it's something that should best be kept between us. It's not good that a boss should be known for showing too much emotion," he said, slipping on his socks and shoes.

"Sure," came the reply. "As you say, you're the boss."

The other team members arrived moments later and Wright stayed long enough to finish his coffee. On his way up the narrow concrete walk that skirted the hotel and led to the street, Wright passed a shadowy figure striding along the walk to the pool. The stranger moved quickly, passed Wright, and then stopped. Probably another visitor who couldn't sleep, Wright thought.

"Hey," the man called out. "Aren't you the guy that owns the whale?"

"Nobody owns whales," Wright said and left the bewildered man to stare at his retreating back.

CHAPTER 11

Acts of Men and God

Wright's voice thundered across the small confines of his marina office. He pivoted in his chair away from the dock-side view of the room's picture window and then sprung to his feet. He leaned over his desk, almost menacingly, and looked at Hoey.

"I don't give a damn about all the optimism in the world. Optimism and good intentions are not going to save that whale. We can hope for the best, but we've got to be ready for the worst. Now let's have that medical report again – this time I want the down side."

"We don't know, and that's the point I'm trying to make," Hoey replied evenly. "Every time we get a blood analysis it shows something different and none of the results pinpoint anything. They do little more than

145

give a general indication of a problem area."

"That's right, Bob," Hyman said. "We have a dozen possibilities of major things that could be affecting that whale's recovery – even killing her. But they're just that – possibilities. We can't tell you what the worst is, or what you call the down side. My belief, and I think Alan will back me on it, is that we should list the possibilities and systematically try treating each one in the order of the gravest importance."

The meeting had been in progress an hour when Hyman suggested the calf be placed on a bland diet. But it was another five hours before Wright felt he had heard enough arguments to accept the plan. Both Wright and the veterinarians knew that a wrong diagnosis and the ensuing treatments could easily kill the whale. It wasn't the last such meeting, but it was significant in the battle for the infant whale's life.

As a result of the meeting, on September 14, the baby was placed on a diet that allowed fish fillets but no whole fish. Three days later the veterinarians announced the intestinal bleeding had stopped and blamed Miracle's previous loss of appetite on an intestinal blockage. For the next week the blood analysis showed a higher than normal white cell count but didn't reveal any other problems. On Tuesday, September 20, almost a month and a half after being rescued from certain death in Menzies Bay, it was announced that Miracle had beaten the effects of her various wounds, including the infection. It was also reported that her diet problem had been solved. If the report was somewhat presumptuous, the veterinarians couldn't be blamed. All the indications showed that she had beaten the enemies within her. By September 24 she was reported to have added a much needed ten inches to her girth and was just an estimated 200 pounds away from a minimum ideal weight of 1,200 pounds.

But the roller coaster ride of gains and setbacks had not been stopped, only slowed temporarily. As soon as the medical-rescue teams surmounted each problem that threatened the calf – believing that they, along with Miracle's help, had conquered the last of the ailments – another crisis would begin. For every six inches of progress there were twelve inches of back- or side-stepping and a yard of medical guesswork. October and November were no less crisis periods than August or September had been. Miracle had always seemed to suffer from problems in her right eye and by the time the year's eleventh month took its place on the calendar the ailment had magnified into a "right now" problem.

External treatments were started on the eye, an act which the veterinarians hoped would circumvent any need for surgery. Medical operations of any type would have been a hazardous undertaking with Miracle for several reasons. Much of what the veterinarians had learned about killer whale medicine had resulted from crisis situations such as Miracle's case, which required quick and often superficial treatment. But this left the veterinarians just on the perimeter of substantial medical knowledge about the animals. Unnecessary probing and a trial-and-error operation with Miracle could have further eroded any progress the baby had made in recovering her health. But one major reason they didn't want to operate – couldn't operate – was because Miracle, like other killer whales, could not be given any type of injectionable anesthetic.

If killer whales, or some other marine mammals, are anesthetized they develop what scientists call a deep-dive syndrome. The anesthetic triggers a nervous reaction in the whale similar to body changes that occur during deep and prolonged dives. All unnecessary or secondary functions are stopped while primary functions, such as heartbeat, are substantially slowed. A deep dive, as it occurs naturally, ends when the whale surfaces to breathe. But for unknown reasons a killer whale cannot regain normal functions, such as breathing, after the syndrome has been produced as a by-product of anesthesia. Killer whales could be anesthetized if they could be "plugged in" to a heart and lung machine that would take over the animal's primary functions until it had sufficiently recovered from the anesthetic. Large machines exist for horses and cows but even those units would not be capable of delivering the vast amount of oxygen needed to support the lungs and life-system of a whale. And such a machine doesn't exist that could be used in the water. To have done an eye operation on a 1,000-pound animal that wasn't under anesthesia would have been impossible.

Fortunately, the external treatments proved effective. And again it was believed the worst was over. However, the medical-rescue team was to learn quickly that the solution to one ailment was often the cause of another problem. Miracle's diet of fish fillets – fish cut in such a way as to eliminate the bones and internal organs – had cured blockages in the stomach and intestinal tract. But, in placing the calf on the easier-to-digest diet, Sealand had unwittingly undercut Miracle's nutritional needs. This act, coupled with the undetermined amount of time Miracle went undernourished in the wild, caused the whale's skin to begin rotting.

At first the medical team believed the skin blemishes to be natural – in fact they were believed to be good signs in much the same way that a mild fever in humans is the sign of the body throwing off infection. Although the condition was worsening, its rate of advance was not readily noticeable to those dealing with Miracle on a day-to-day basis. It was Wright who, after an absence of three weeks, recognized the degree to which the whale's skin condition was deteriorating.

Not only were the veterinarians called on to make a diagnosis but provincial and federal government dietitians were asked for recommendations. Following the meetings Miracle was placed back on a whole-fish herring diet. Although that particular diet had caused problems during the calf's early recovery, her stomach had matured sufficiently in the meantime to readily accept and process the meatier diet. And just to be sure she was getting all the vital nutrients this time, Sealand placed the baby whale on a massive dose of vitamins. It was the same dose as given an eight-times-larger male killer whale at Sealand, and that dosage was double the amount given killer whales in many other oceanariums.

Although Miracle's skin continued to peel off in large patches it was with clear, healthy skin showing underneath. Areas that had been described in daily medical reports as looking like cottage cheese, healed quickly under the vitamin-enriched, whole-fish program. It was later discovered that the antibiotics and drugs used to treat Miracle's other ailments also partially contributed to the calf's early stomach disorders.

During the same period – October through November – Miracle was also plagued by worms and parasites. The condition had been evident since the early days of rescue but the calf's wounds and other ailments had been given necessary priority, and again the medical-rescue team faced the inevitable dilemma of curing one set of problems only to compound another. Miracle's enriched diet had not only benefitted her but added vigour to the worms and parasites. In mid-November, when all the calf's other life-threatening problems seemed to be under control, the veterinarians began attacking the internal intruders with two worming agents. Not only were an estimated 1,500 worms put to a final rest but an undetermined amount of parasites, which had begun to lay eggs in Miracle's blubber areas, were forced to flee by squirming out through the calf's skin.

*   *   *

Not all the action involving the whale was taking place at the recovery pool, though. While the medical-rescue teams worked through the summer and into the fall and winter to ensure Miracle's recovery, Sealand administrators began the final stages of planning for the calf's permanent home at Sealand. Construction began a week before Christmas. The plan was to add a separate but adjoining sixty-by-forty-eight-foot enclosure to the end of the existing killer whale pool at the oceanarium. Miracle's home below water was made of a heavy-gauge vinyl-coated wire mesh, which allowed the flow of tidal water into the pool. By February the construction crew had finished all but the final touches of paint and above-water superstructure.

During the early and middle stages of Miracle's recovery, four eight-hour shifts, of four people each, stood guard over the calf at the hotel pool. By mid-November the baby whale had improved enough so that only one person remained on each of the shifts. By the time the pool had been finished in late February the calf had lived through sixty successive days without enduring any medical crisis. There was one event, however, that Sealand staffers logged as a crisis, even though Miracle was oblivious to its threat.

Despite Victoria's reputation for a mild climate, there is usually at least one storm during the winter that sweeps around from the outside water of the North Pacific to ravage the passages and beaches of the inside waters between Vancouver Island and British Columbia mainland. If the winds howl into the confines of Juan de Fuca Strait and then shift almost 180 degrees (as they sometimes do in the island-studded waters off southern Vancouver Island), the storm will unleash its direct threat at Oak Bay.

On January 24, 1978, just such a storm began forming. With freakish and alarming speed the storm formed its nucleus and fought off several other systems starting on the island's west coast. It shoved its way along the shoreline, moving southward into the bottle-neck of Juan de Fuca Strait. Its force was multiplied in the channel and tons of water, not able to escape the on-slaught, were pushed into twenty-foot-high rollers which careened madly through the strait. The storm had built and moved so rapidly that Environment Canada had been unable to issue their normal twenty-four-hour, twelve- or even six-hour storm warnings. When they did realize what was happening they weren't able to get a fix on the boiling mass long enough to determine its strength. To make matters worse the wind drove in on the heels of the highest tides of the month which in this case doubled the height of the tides in early January.

The rise and fall of tides in Oak Bay regularly lapped their way up and down Miracle's pool wall, which bordered the beach, so it was of little concern to the lone rescue team member working the graveyard shift when the tide began to creep up the wall. He noticed the rising water with the same consciousness as he accepted the light breeze that ruffled the surface of the pool and the bay beyond. These conditions were not unusual, and he had been trained to watch for the critically abnormal. Even the brisk southeast wind a couple of hours later was no reason to sound any alarms. The winds were whipping the tide-pushed water into medium-sized rolling waves that crashed against the concrete wall and shot wind-driven spray into the pool. But by 4:00 that Tuesday morning the attendant had roused Matthews from bed – the tide was continuing to rise and the occasional wave was leaping the wall and pouring itself into the pool.

On the way out the door Matthews tapped the glass of a barometer that hung in his living-room. The needle plummetted, almost to the bottom of the scale, and he cursed through an exhale of breath. By the time he and three other team members, who had been alerted, donned skin suits – a warm type of diving suit – the tide was nearing its nine-foot peak, but the wind was still mounting, heading for a high of eighty miles an hour. Seeing that Miracle was still safe – at least for the moment – the team turned its efforts to anchoring down a makeshift plywood hut at the edge of the pool. During the summer months it had been little more than a canvas tarp stretched over posts to protect the medical-rescue teams from the sun. As the crisp chills of autumn had moved into the body-numbing winds of winter the canvas had been replaced by random sheets of plywood. Eventually a sliding glass door and an electric heater were added. Slowly the shack had come to house the oddities of medical equipment, food and charts necessary to maintain the baby whale. When Matthews and the other team members arrived the lone attendant was standing on the leeward side of the hut struggling to keep the structure upright against the shuddering blows of the gusting wind. And even then the gusts were managing to lift the seaward edge of the shack several inches off the ground.

After the shack had been anchored with sandbags the team shut down the two pumps that ran continuously to keep Miracle's pool filled. Matthews had ordered them stopped because the intake lines, lodged on the bottom of the bay sixty feet from shore, had begun sucking up sand that was being whirled about by the storm-ravaged waters. Although during the summer it took both pumps operating at near full speed to maintain the five-foot water depth within the six-foot-deep enclosure, the waves that now poured over the pool's seaward wall kept pace with the amount of water continuously seeping from the ancient structure's many leaks. By 8:00 the intensity of the storm and height of the waves had increased so much that the water level began to rise. The level had always been kept a foot below the top of the walls; first as a safety precaution in case the pool had to be drained rapidly for an emergency, and second because no one was sure that the cracking pool walls could stand the pressure of a full load of water.

As the waves pouring into the pool continued to grow larger and stronger in force, and the inside water level kept rising dangerously close to the top edge of the pool, Matthews began to worry that either a wall would collapse or that Miracle would be sucked over the wall by the undertow. One of the team members, an experienced diver, volunteered to dive to the bottom of the wall on the storm-lashed seaward side of the pool to open the closed drain valve. Matthews agreed, reluctantly, after the diver agreed to wear a safety harness that tethered him umbilically to mother earth. It was a precaution – a life-line – to keep the diver from being dragged to sea in the turbulent undercurrents. It was the only safety measure Matthews could offer – the diver would have to take his own precautions against being dashed against the wall by the incoming rollers.

The volunteer waited for the legendary seventh wave to pass – supposedly the largest and strongest wave in a series of seven that occurs during a storm. He jumped feet first into the trough between waves and managed to press his bulk against the wall before the next roller crashed into place. He let his lead weight-belt carry him down between incoming waves, timing his descent according to the submarine suck and heaves. When a wave approached he would press his body tightly against the wall, minimizing his chance of being smashed against the concrete. Though it was less than a dozen feet to the bottom he had to pin himself to the wall three times before he reached his target. He made his ascent the same way.

Even the fully opened valve failed to drain the pool to a safe level. By 10:00 A.M. the storm had reached its peak. During the night the powerful undercurrents had sucked logs and driftwood off nearby beaches and they were now being hurled into the pool, posing a greater threat to the baby whale than the rising water level and undercurrents. The team took turns forming a human wall to protect Miracle. They straddled the outer wall in pairs, fighting the currents and winds in an effort to catch the storm-tossed wood before it reached the pool. Somewhat confused by the commotion, but not aware of any real danger, Miracle lay at the surface beside one of the side walls. She was away from the direct threat of

the undertow although she could have been hit at any given moment by logs which were landing randomly throughout the pool before being pushed by waves to the far shallow corner.

After most of the storm-tossed logs had been caught and stacked on shore, Matthews again turned his attention to the overflowing pool. The beachside wall had begun to show the strain of the storm's pressure. Each thunderous wave that was brought to a halt against the old wall caused it to shudder visibly. Matthews used the hotel lobby phone – both the telephone and electrical connections at poolside had been washed out – to contact Oak Bay Marina manager Wayne Wagner. He pleaded with Wagner to have the largest pump he could find delivered to the pool. Wagner's office was located on the westerly side of a building complex that sprawled along the Oak Bay Marina foreshore. The marina itself was in the hollow of two breakwaters and an island. Amid a stack of paperwork that columned each side of his desk Wagner was in a comparable pocket of calm. He was sure that Matthews was exaggerating the conditions and decided the half-mile drive would be worth the effort, to make sure of the situation. He never even climbed out of his car when he viewed the pool from the hotel parking lot, but jammed the vehicle into a squealing reverse, turned around, and sped back to the marina.

The pump was delivered within an hour – rented from an excavation firm complete with an engineer capable of deciphering a mass of dials that peppered one side of the machine. The snarling metal beast, with its octopus arms of hoses, remains in Matthews' memory as the largest pump he'd ever seen. Set on its own trailer wheels the unit reached more than six feet from the ground and was designed to pump more than 1,100 gallons a minute. Yet, even at that rate, the pump had to be worked at full speed for over four hours to lower the water level six inches. Gradually the wind began to abate.

By 1:00 that afternoon the tide had turned, inching its way down the outer wall in retreat from the scarred battleground. And, as usually happens along the island's coast, the wind slackened at the same time and then shifted a full 180 degrees so that it blew harmlessly over the land from the northwest. Again, Miracle and her friends had emerged victors over perilous odds. It took a full day to clear the area of the wreckage – logs had been hurled a hundred feet from the seaward edge of the pool – but the team firmly believed the storm was the last of a long list of crises that had confronted both them and Miracle.

CHAPTER 12

Sky Rider

Neither Matthews, Wright, nor the rest or the medical-rescue team wanted to risk Miracle to another of the winter storms, so plans, already under way to move the calf, were given absolute priority. Yet the question of just how to move the baby whale was causing some concerned head scratching. Because the winter rains had created a slippery mud surface beneath the lawns surrounding the recovery pool, the truck and crane used to lower Miracle into the enclosure couldn't be used to retrieve her. In total, a move by truck would have entailed the use of two massive cranes – one at each pool – and would have left Miracle out of her water element for an hour and a half. The degree of stress inflicted upon a killer whale, and thus the success of a move, is directly related to the amount of time the animal is withheld from its natural environment. An hour and a half moving time seemed, to all concerned, to be stretching the limits of luck just a shade thin.

Another plan – which was less costly and would have had Miracle out of the water for a more acceptable period of an hour – was to place a crane on a barge. The barge would then be snuggled between the outlying reefs seaward of the recovery pool and, once the calf was tethered safely at the end of the crane's boom, the entire rig would be towed the half-mile to Sealand, and the whale lowered into her new pool. In theory it was a good idea and had the operation been scheduled for the summer months it probably would have proved itself in practice. There was a force to reckon with, however, that made a move by barge in February impractical, if not foolhardy. If a sudden winter storm, such as the one just past, were to suddenly occur, a barge moored precariously between the reefs outside the pool wouldn't stand a sailor's chance of surviving the onslaught of waters that could sink an ocean-going ship, and a whale calf tethered to the crane boom would be doomed to an unsightly and painful death amid splintering wood and twisting steel.

Les Wood was scoffed at when he offered a third alternative – employment of a helicopter to make the move. Wright wanted no part of such a daring and, as far as killer whales are concerned, unproven method of transporting Miracle. Matthews, realizing that their choice of options was becoming slim to the point of non-existent, decided to investigate the idea further. After searching out the largest and most reputable air craft charter firm he made several trips to the mainland to gain first-hand knowledge of the "chopper's" capabilities, and more important, its incapabilities. Within two weeks he learned that renting a machine was less expensive than the previous alternatives would have been, and he was convinced that weather was less of a deterrent to a rotary aircraft than to a tug and barge.

The one big question, and at best one that could only be guessed at, was, how would Miracle react to being airlifted? To find out just what the calf would have to endure, Matthews arranged to stand under a hovering helicopter. He learned, to his surprise, that there was little noise and virtually no down-draft directly under the aircraft. The tell-tale, cracking-whip sound is caused by the rotor tips breaking the sound barrier and precedes the machine, while the exhaust noise of the engines is vented to the rear. All of this leaves the undercarriage of the machine reasonably quiet. The huge volume of air forced into a down-draft by the rotors is pushed down and away from the aircraft in the form of a cone, again leaving the undercarriage virtually untouched by the goings on above. Matthews came away with the idea that Miracle would find the sensation little different to being fastened in a sling at the end of a crane boom. But the fact that convinced Matthews of the helicopter's ultimate practicality for the move was that the flight time, from pickup until Miracle was touched down in her new pool, would be less than ten minutes.

It took another week to convince Wright of the plan and even when he nodded his approval it was with the resignation of a man who knew there were no other options. Because of his sensitivity to the situation and the fact that Matthews had already gained extensive knowledge of helicopter transportation, Wright also agreed to be no more than a spectator during the transfer. It was an agreement necessary to keep Wright's

161

infectious emotionalism from destroying what Matthews knew had to be a meticulously timed and faultlessly executed operation.

On Monday, February 27, the sun rose above Juan de Fuca Strait in a cold, orange ball. It wasn't until mid-morning that its rays began to push any warmth through the cloudless sky. At 8:30 A.M., a large twin-engined single rotor helicopter landed on a sectioned-off area of the Sealand parking lot. The machine's touchdown was the culmination of three weeks' organization and labour yet was only preliminary to the tense, hustling activity that was to envelop the remainder of that morning.

At 8:40 A.M., the tall, heavy set and mutton-chop-adorned pilot was included in a final briefing of more than sixty Sealand personnel. Many of the staff had been specially employed for the occasion to help control the expected crowds in the area. Each member was given a sheet of written instructions and then they were individually read out from a master sheet so that everyone became familiar with every facet of the operation. A freelance writer, who attended the meeting as part of an assignment to cover the story for *National Geographic* magazine, later likened the machine precision and fanatic attention to detail in the meeting to a paranoid plot to overthrow the government. But Matthews and the other managerial staff at Sealand weren't about to leave anything to chance.

During the preceding weeks, attention to detail had become a way of life at the oceanarium and the surrounding marina. The helicopter firm had sent in their own safety manager and under his guidance Matthews' crew had seen to such things as the securing of boats and nearby dinghys, the laborious task of clearing the surrounding beach area of small pieces of driftwood and the sweeping of the designated landing area. Everything that was loose both inside and around the oceanarium was tied down to prevent it from being thrown around in the air-wash of the helicopter's rotors.

After the briefing the blue-jacketed Sealand staff took up their specified positions. The medical team rushed to do a final medical on Miracle at the hotel pool and they were joined by the rescue team designated to that area of operations. At both the hotel enclosure and the Sealand pool, iron scaffolding had been erected. The ten-foot-high structure at the recovery pool was designed to hold the sling-encased whale calf out of the water in readiness for the cable hook-up from the helicopter while the scaffolding at Sealand had been built for use in the event of an emergency, during which the calf had to be held out of the water. When the results of the medical were known – showing the best-ever blood count – Miracle and the sling were hoisted clear of the recovery pool and suspended from the scaffolding.

Wright had kept his promise during the morning. It took a great effort on his part but he managed to keep from interfering in the operation. Actually he didn't arrive on the scene until an hour after all things had been put into motion. Yet his silence was not to be marked as passive detachment. He gnarled his way through a box of fifty toothpicks – his one concession to a recent decision to quit cigarette smoking. The toothpicks jumped nimbly around his mouth, over his teeth and across his tongue. During exceedingly tense moments one lasted less than a minute before it was desecrated under a vengeful gnashing of teeth. Matthews was so impressed with the performance that he sent for a reserve packet of the wood slivers, knowing fully that they represented the slender line between Wright's unwanted involvement and his spectatorship.

After half an hour of muted watching Wright broke the silence with his one and only demand of the day.

"I want to meet the guy who's going to drop the whale," he said to Matthews, while shoving two toothpicks into his mouth.

When the two men reached the Sealand parking lot the pilot was walking unconcernedly around the seaward edge of the black-topped area, casting unhurried looks to the sea beyond. A large, shiny metal vacuum flask was clamped tightly under his right arm and he used his left hand to raise the flask's metal top-cum-cup to his mouth in long, luxuriant sips of whatever it contained. Before Matthews could point out the pilot, Wright had begun striding towards a blue-suited man, standing nervously rigid beside the helicopter. It didn't take long for Wright to learn that this capable looking man was not the pilot but the co-pilot. When he asked where he could find the aircraft's skipper, and the man at the seaward end of the parking lot was pointed out, Wright shoved another toothpick into his mouth – bringing the total to three – and bellowed out Matthews' name, miraculously keeping the toothpicks in place at the same time.

Matthews had to admit the pilot looked a little unconventional. His baggy brown flight coveralls certainly looked like they would be better suited to an auto mechanic. His peaked red hat – that seemed to be the colour under the dirt – looked like it had been rescued from a little league garage sale and his mutton chop sideburns made the middle-aged man appear as a likely candidate for a straight man part in a nightclub comic duo. There was nothing in his looks or his movements that hastened to instil confidence in his ability, although Matthews was quick to point out to Wright that the man had successfully flown the craft the twenty-two-mile distance from Vancouver and had landed it safely.

"But he wasn't drinking from that flask then, was he?" Wright said as he watched the pilot pour another cupful from the shiny container. "I hope to heaven that he's drinking coffee out of that thing."

Wright's confidence in the pilot's capabilities was not enhanced several minutes later, when, after a signal from the ground-stationed communications man, the pilot walked over to the helicopter. Halfway there he tripped over the static lines that were draped on the ground around the machine and when he began his climb into the cockpit he smashed his head against the door frame. Wright moaned so loudly that at least half of the thousand people gathered in the area turned to look at him. Matthews didn't attempt to stop Wright's wounded-moose noise – he too was becoming concerned about the pilot's ability to carry out the job.

Several minutes after the pilot had entered the cockpit there was a whirring of action inside the machine and the four-bladed propeller began to whip through an increasingly faster arc. The machine remained squatted on the pavement, growling, whining, and pushing out dust clouds from the ground for about five minutes before a thumbs-up signal from the safety manager gave the pilot clearance to take-off. He hovered the machine momentarily above the parking lot to test the zephyr that was beginning to blow in off the water. As in the case of most propeller-driven aircraft, the air movement was looked upon as an asset by the pilot. A slight wind in the right direction – and this breeze couldn't have been better had it been tailored – gave the pilot a counter-force to push against when the craft was put into the hover position. He flopped the helicopter from side to side, dropped the tail, then lowered the nose slightly to get the all-important feel of the conditions. And then with little effort the craft peeled off sideways to stop abruptly over the Sealand whale pool. It was a test to see how the machine reacted to all the conditions that would be imposed on it, and the pilot, more professional than he looked, was doing his best to eliminate the possibility of all the surprises he could.

The helicopter was once again landed on the parking lot but this time the rotors continued to beat out their idling rhythm and the pilot stayed in the cockpit. After overseeing the trial run, both the communications officer, armed with a sophisticated walkie-talkie, and the safety manager, drove to the hotel pool. The machine continued to idle on the parking lot for half an hour and then, as the medical-rescue team began to bundle Miracle into the sling, the communications officer radioed the pilot to take up a hovering position over a pair of islands a mile seaward of the bay.

Miracle was somewhat curious about the commotion in the pool but she wasn't tense or concerned about the activity. Throughout the morning she swam easily and strongly around the enclosure in the counter-clockwise direction which had become her custom. She really believed the rubber-suited people who splashed through the water to carry out their tasks were put there for her enjoyment, and had begun to use her strengthening tail playfully knocking the feet from under each team member who ventured into the pool. The game became so intense on Miracle's part that Matthews had to send in a decoy. One of the crew members was given a bucket of herring and ordered to keep the calf's attention. The food and the ensuing back and stomach rub were so tempting to Miracle that she cast only a random glance at the workers.

Bill Davis, who had arrived earlier that morning, threw a paper cup into a litter basket outside the fence spectator barrier and exercised his privilege of freedom by going back to the edge of the pool. He wore a tag with the logo of Sealand and his name printed on it – a pass system developed for the occasion to keep all but a few authorized spectators from infiltrating the off-bounds working areas around both pools. The paper cup had contained coffee – Davis's sixth cup of the morning. The steamy liquid was the only thing he had drunk or eaten aside from the two pieces of toast he had reluctantly choked down for breakfast. Still, his stomach was in a knot as if he had swallowed something that had fought off all attempts at digestion and was lying in a heavy lump. He had nervously spent the morning walking the half-mile between the two pools trying to watch everything that was happening and trying to understand the preparations which appeared on the surface to be little more than a mass of entangled bodies in a state of confusion. He spent little time with Miracle since most of his time seemed to be spent in motion between and around the pools. It was only a half effective measure against his mounting nervousness.

Nevertheless Davis kept his misgivings to himself and his emergence at one pool and then the other, and the walks between, went unnoticed by meandering spectators or the medical-rescue teams. At the point that Miracle had been lifted from the water and secured in her sling from the scaffolding overhanging the hotel pool he retreated to Sealand to await the calf's arrival there.

Shortly after Davis's unnoticed departure from the hotel pool the already hustling activity in that area became intense. A runner from the Sealand pool notified Matthews that all equipment and manpower at that end was ready. Several hundred yards into the bay from the recovery pool a Royal Canadian Mounted Police cruiser had its sleek blue hull jockeyed into a standby position. Its duty was twofold: to keep the area clear of boats that might be capsized by the helicopter's downdraft and, should anything go wrong with the airlift, two divers on board were prepared to cut Miracle free from the sling. On shore a squad of Oak Bay policemen had blocked off the half-mile of road between the two pools. Several policemen stood sentry at each pool to deal with any over-reaction from the growing crowds. At the end of a side street that butted against the hotel property a squad car, its red emergency light flashing, sat idling in front of the Sealand pickup truck. The constable, detailed to drive the police cruiser, sat sideways inside the car with the door open and his feet resting on the ground. He waited anxiously for the sound of the helicopter and then the sight of the running rescue team. Mentally he traced the route to Sealand and hoped his duty to run interference for the crew, who would be in the truck behind him, would remain more of a precaution than a necessity.

When a final check had been made, and all systems and personnel were reported on standby alert, it was 10:30 A.M. The communications officer lifted the bulky two-way radio to his mouth and ordered the helicopter into "action station one." Within seconds the machine was hovering over the rocks along the seaward edge of the pool. The co-pilot activated an electric winch on the underside of the helicopter, which deployed a hundred

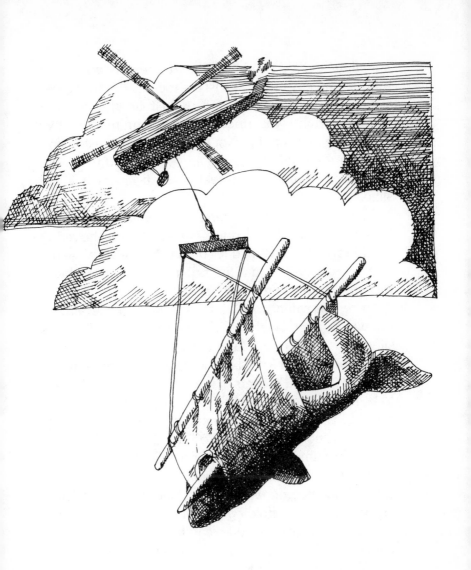

and fifty feet of cable. When fully extended it was bumped several times against the rocks to discharge any static electricity that had been built up through the rotors. Wright was unconsciously annihilating five toothpicks at this point. Not having had any instruction in the fine art of helicopter flying, he winced when the cable was dropped sixty feet away from the waiting sling.

"The whale is over here, you idiots!" he raged through the wind and noise created by the hovering machine. It was several days before Matthews was able to convince Wright that the hook and cable had been dropped onto the rocks for a purpose.

Once the safety manager had deemed the aircraft drained of all static electricity, the hook-up to Miracle's sling was fast, smooth, and accurate – with one minor exception. One of four six-foot ground-pull ropes, which dangled from the corners of the sling, and would allow it to be pulled into position as it was suspended above the Sealand pool, had become caught in the scaffolding. While the communications officer deluged the radio with a breathless stream of orders Matthews worked feverishly and precariously to untangle the line. For the sake of balance he worked with one foot on the sling and one on the scaffolding, but when the line was jerked free he found his stance spreading rapidly as the sling began to drift away from the platform.

"All of a sudden I was faced with a decision and three alternatives. Ten feet below were the rocks and cement along the shallow end of the pool – I couldn't have ended the fall on my feet even on the wings of a prayer, so I was sure to get some broken bones and worse, if my head hit first. I could jump for the sling and, surmising I made the leap safely, I could have tagged along for the ride. I wasn't too keen on that. Or I could try to get both feet back on the scaffolding. That was the idea I liked best but it was becoming more improbable each second since my foot was hooked over the edge of the sling and it didn't give me anything solid to push against."

Just as Matthews was becoming convinced that a jump to the sling would be the only relatively safe solution to the predicament, a gust of wind blew both the helicopter and sling a foot closer to the scaffolding. It was all Matthews needed. Once safely back on the platform he waved a signal to the communications officer and Miracle's sling streamed off obediently beneath the helicopter.

"We have lift-off," the communications officer said unemotionally to the helicopter pilot. "Proceed on schedule to action station two. Land – repeat – land on instruction only."

The communications officer then joined other staff around the pool in making a dash for Sealand. The medical-rescue team, including Matthews and Wright, didn't have much time to watch the take-off as they made a dash for the truck and two other cars. Although another team was ready to receive the calf at the Sealand pool, the recovery pool team didn't want to miss the splashdown if they could help it. As the team climbed into the vehicles and sped away from the hotel, the leading policeman radioed for clearance from other patrolmen along the route. All public traffic had been kept off the road for two hours but an elderly woman, whose house was on the edge of the barricaded roadway, didn't so much as glance for oncoming traffic when she backed out of her driveway, little more than a hundred feet in front of the speeding police car. At the same time that the constable put the car into a braking skid he punched the siren button. Having prodded her little car in the same direction as the police cruiser the lady cast hurried glances into her rear-view mirror, but refused to pull over. Her nervousness showed in her driving. She continually let the little car weave across the centre line, especially when the police car made any attempt to pass.

Fortunately the route was short. Matthews thought out loud that at least they would be able to put both themselves and the old lady out of their respective miseries when the cavalcade entered the approaching turn into the Sealand parking lot. No such luck. Completely unnerved by the wailing siren and flashing red lights, the woman swung the car sharply into the parking lot entrance and stopped, thinking she was safe. When the police car skidded around her car and over the sidewalk she threw up her hands and fainted. The pickup truck, not as manoeuvrable as the police car, bounced over the sidewalk but failed to miss a garden. The next two cars made the turn but Wright's low-slung Mercedes Coupé left a muffler to mark the spot.

By no means were the troublesome events over when the vehicles stopped at the sidewalk entrance to Sealand. In his hurry to make up for lost time Matthews jumped from the truck and wrenched his foot against the curb. The pain was later diagnosed as a torn ligament but initially unaware of its name, cause or seriousness, he hobbled after the other team members. The helicopter pilot, watching the progress of the medical-rescue crew, had slowed the craft's approach to the oceanarium, allowing the crew to reach the area ahead of the whale.

On deck at Sealand a small crowd had gathered

around the pool to watch the calf as it approached through a sharp blaze of morning sun. The winter sun was low and its blinding rays were reflected by the water as it shone across the bay. Davis had to squint his looks at the highflying calf yet he saw enough to add to his agitation. Miracle's tail flukes, hanging a full six feet out of the back of the sling, were swinging from side to side in quick snaps that revealed the calf's fright. It looked for all the world as if the whale would wiggle itself free of the sling to plunge backwards into a hundred-foot drop to the sea. Wright was just as tense. There were no toothpicks visible in his mouth but loud wood-splintering crunches were evidence that the oceanarium boss hadn't yet given up the habit.

Matthews learned later that Miracle's struggles in the sling were not as much from fright as they were a reaction to a strobe effect of sunlight passing through the whipping blades of the rotor. The calf, unable to see anything through the sling below or beside her, became acutely aware of the strange light. Her struggles had been an effort to turn herself on her side so she could search for the cause of this peculiar phenomenon.

While the helicopter and whale made their final approach, the recovery pool team joined the Sealand based crew in making last second preparations. Divers simultaneously strapped on air tanks and weight belts before plunging into the forty-foot-deep pool. A sixteen-foot dinghy was launched into the enclosure and several men jumped aboard. Other members took up predesignated posts along the edge of the pool. As the helicopter hovered into position, suspending the baby whale fifty feet above the pool, the first effects of the downdrafts were felt. The pool was surrounded by a ten-foot-high wall, which served to trap the incoming blasts of air. Soon the wind speed was in excess of fifty miles an hour. The surface of the pool was whipped into waves that angrily heaved the dinghy back and forth.

Slowly the helicopter descended with its cargo, finally touching the sling to the water precisely on target. On deck, television crews and newspaper photographers moved in for better shots while the men in the boat were pulled into position via ropes from the bow and stern. Matthews signalled the communications officer to have the sling lowered another foot so that the whale would be partially submerged in the water. Divers moved closer, both to steady the sling with the ground-pull ropes, and to grab the calf if she got caught up in the sling or later started to sink. One side of the sling was dropped on cue. The divers peeled it from around the calf and once she was pushed from the edge of the pool, the pilot was signalled to take the mass of sheepskin and pipes to deck level. It was then that the hook was released from the sling's crossbar and the helicopter freed to land in the parking lot. The move from lift-off to touchdown had taken six minutes and ten seconds. The flight time was a record in itself but the move was more than that – it was an event marking history. Never before had a killer whale been transported by helicopter.

CHAPTER 13

Miracle Worker

Bill Davis had long been touted as the "Miracle Worker" by the press but he was never so pushed to prove the title as he was on the afternoon of Wednesday, March 1.

The days leading up to that particular afternoon – Monday, Tuesday, and Wednesday morning – had started with hope and ended with desperation. The first event of those days had been Miracle's helicopter transfer, which in itself had been nothing less than a runaway success. It had been covered by the press, including a major Toronto newspaper, it formed the basis for a *National Geographic* children's story, and spurred a television documentary. Radio stations covered it with blow-by-blow descriptions, and those people who didn't want second-hand information crowded the spectator areas around both pools to glimpse the historic flight.

But Miracle threw a curve at her rescuers and in retrospect many people believed it was because the rescuers had unwittingly thrown a curve at her. Minutes after being released into the new pool Monday the calf went into shock. She swam the perimeter halfway around the pool and stopped to huddle herself in one corner. Instead of marvelling at man's ingenuity Davis retreated from the pool in the company of fear and guilt. He had not been witness to any of Miracle's previous setbacks. He had been phoned and told about them but he had never actually seen the pathetic convulsions that had wracked the whale. He was afraid she wouldn't live through the spasms that now gripped her body. He also felt with recurring guilt, that maybe all he had succeeded in doing was to have prolonged the calf's agony.

He was quiet during the four-hour return drive to Campbell River later that Monday. Lois broke the silence only occasionally, knowing that her husband needed the time to sort the flow of thoughts and feelings that were crammed into his mind. She too had many of the same feelings but as a woman she was free to deal with them more openly than her husband. She could talk about them, weep about them. Her husband's process was much more complicated. He needed first to identify the feelings and thoughts and then file them into emotional categories. After that came a process of familiarization which served to take the hurt out of the emotions. Only then could they be brought out in the open.

*   *   *

Throughout the day divers had been stationed in and around the pool. Medical teams put on duty at poolside were spelled off in six-hour shifts. Many of the Sealand and medical staff not scheduled for shifts during the night stayed on anyway, helping what little they could, watching and hoping like all the other people gathered around the pool. It was a cold, damp night. There were no clouds to hold in the warmth of the day and the bitter-sweet of the seashore was held to earth heavily under the cold air. The distant reach of the sparkling stars seemed only to further chill the dampness. Conversations erupted for short periods in the lonely silence but they were strained and contained only half-thoughts. All senses were essentially trained on the calf. Everyone was waiting, hoping for that break that would signal the end of the whale's latest crisis.

There is little to describe of Miracle that day and night. She didn't sleep. Her body was gripped in waves of shakes and shivers and grotesque contortions. Perhaps Hoey said it best when he turned away from the baby after a particularly bad period of spasms and referred to her condition as "her own private hell." Yet Hoey was carrying his own set of demons – even as a disciple of modern medicine he couldn't extricate Miracle from the hellish ailments that plagued her, and that realization ate at him.

The rising sun Tuesday morning brought little in the way of warmth. Although the day had been born bright and cloudless, a mounting winter wind began driving the chill deeper, through clothing into wearied bones. Miracle, still in a state of shock that continued to keep her huddled in one corner of the pool, had refused all attempts to feed her.

A little less than twenty hours earlier Miracle's shock

and refusal to eat didn't overly concern the medical-rescue crews. It had been a disappointment – everyone had hoped that the calf would make the pool transfer without any problems – but no one became overly worried when shock did set in. It was normal, particularly in an animal so young. Everyone involved with the medical-rescue team knew that killer whales were susceptible to shock when moved around outside their element, and that any reaction could throw a whale off its eating patterns. The anxieties had formed and grown Monday night. By Tuesday morning there was no doubt in anyone's mind that the calf was in the midst of a serious relapse. The shock should have diminished and the whale should have started regaining her appetite. Instead, she continued to huddle in one corner of the pool, occasionally emitting long, moaning squeals and refusing both food and attention.

By noon Tuesday, Hoey ordered a medical. It was easy to draw the necessary blood – too easy. Miracle never moved. Yet the results later that day showed that the calf was normal, healthy in every respect. It left only one conclusion – her state of shock was not being caused by physical disruptions but by a state of mental depression. Before she could be helped the medical team had to find the cause. At first the airlift was blamed, but slowly that theory was abandoned. There had been no circumstance in the flight that Miracle hadn't faced before – several times. Her overland trip from Menzies Bay had been far longer and, having been the calf's first experience with man-made transportation, had been more taxing than the short helicopter flight.

The agonies of the situation continued through Tuesday night with one stirring revelation – a reasonable diagnosis had been made about the cause of Miracle's shock. It was Sealand's animal trainer Cees Schrage who first began to understand the whale calf's problem. As the medical-rescue teams packed the deck surrounding the pool Schrage noticed the calf still retained a curiosity about events and people around her. She ignored the advances of divers in the pool – in fact she ignored everything within the pool. The reason for her shock, then, had to be the enclosure, he told the crew. "She is afraid of the pool."

Miracle's recovery pool at the hotel – where she had died and had been revived and where she had surmounted dozens of life-draining ordeals – was small and comfortably familiar. With a deep end of five feet, a shallow end that angled out of the water like a rocky beach, the hotel pool had been Miracle's home for more than a third of her life. It had helped form the transition from the cruelty she had experienced in the wild to the kindness she had found in her final station with man.

In comparison, the new pool was twenty times the size of the concrete recovery pool and the new home was open to the ocean, separated only by layers of wire mesh. Also, for the first time in probably a year, Miracle heard the sounds of another killer whale, who was lodged in the pool next to her. And it had been the corner of her own pool that was next to the neighbouring whale pool to which Miracle had gravitated. The experience of contact with another whale and the forty-foot depth of the pool – in which Miracle refused to submerge – was too much for the baby to deal with.

Schrage had a plan. He had noticed Miracle watching the movements of Haida, her male killer whale neighbour, and thought he might spark the baby's interest and get her to respond by engaging in activities with the other whale. Schrage kept Haida awake for the remainder of the night, exaggerating all his actions – especially the feeding process. But, despite his best efforts, Wednesday morning approached without Miracle having shown the slightest response toward feeding or efforts to make her venture from her corner. She continued to be wracked by intermittent spasms.

"We're going to lose her if we don't get some food into her soon and find some way to reverse the shock," Wright said as the changing duty shifts mustered shortly before dawn.

He hadn't said anything that wasn't already known by everyone.

"Damn it!" he said in an explosion of frustration that was punctuated by a punch at the plywood wall behind him.

He turned and walked away from the crew, slowly pacing the length of Miracle's pool. He was halfway back when he picked up the pace to a trot and began shouting.

"We've got one more chance – there's one ace left in the deck. Matthews, phone Davis and have him get here as soon as possible. I don't care what he's doing or how it affects his job. We need him here. If there's any problems get back to me and I'll talk to his boss."

Davis got Matthews' call several minutes before he was to leave for work. Five minutes later he was heading for Victoria. He arrived at Sealand shortly after noon and began a crucial probe of the bond between himself and Miracle.

At first Davis did little more than talk to the whale calf while he leaned over the edge of the pool to rub her gently with a sponge. Miracle was responsive. She rolled on her back to have her stomach rubbed and playfully pushed at Davis's shoulders. When he stood up away from her an hour later she vocalized shrilly, much more intensely and forcefully than she had wailed and moaned earlier in the day. Davis then asked for an aluminum dinghy to be launched into the enclosure, and he paddled into the middle of the pool.

For two hours Davis tried to entice Miracle to centre pool with offerings of herring. Miracle was obviously still fighting her fear of the pool. She thrashed in her corner every time Davis slapped a fish on the water or called out to her, but her emotional blockage kept her from accepting the offers. Davis began to concede defeat, not because he was weary, but because his efforts had worked Miracle into such an agitated state that he was frightened any more pressure would push the baby into mental collapse – possibly killing her. But when he tried to leave the pool he was met by an angry Wright.

"What the hell do you think you're doing? You're the only chance she's got, and you're pulling up stakes," Wright yelled.

"I'm going to kill her if I keep it up," Davis protested.

"And what do you think is going to happen to her if you leave? If she's lucky enough not to starve to death the shock will eat at her an inch at a time. Either way she'll go slowly and painfully."

Wright watched the impact of his words as they registered on Davis's face, and then he lowered his voice.

"Without you, Miracle would have never come this far, Bill. You can't give up now. I know I'm asking you to do the hardest thing of your life. It's true, she may die from the anxiety but she will die if we don't try. We haven't got any choices left and you're the only person who can bring her back."

Davis looked away from Wright to meet the reluctant gaze of Hoey. The veterinarian remained silent and just

181

nodded his head. Davis was silent for a moment, standing in the boat at the edge of the pool. He looked at the now sleek form of Miracle, her wounds almost invisible, and remembered what she had looked like that first day in Menzies Bay. He took a deep breath.

"All right," he whispered and shoved the boat back to centre pool.

Miracle reacted even more violently to his urgings this time, heaving the water around her into a saline foam. The process continued unabated for half an hour until Davis asked if he could try another approach. After outlining it to Wright and Hoey he paddled the skiff to within three feet of the calf. When she came up beside the boat, open-mouthed, he dropped herring down her gullet. A few minutes later he pushed the boat several feet closer to centre pool, urging Miracle to follow for a further feed of fish, but she refused. An hour later, at Wright's urging, he paddled the boat to the other side of the pool to take a rest.

The calf was silent as Davis made his way across the pool and she intently watched his every move. When the skiff had been tied in place Davis shipped the oars and turned sideways in his seat – with his back to the whale – so that he could grasp the deck to climb out of the boat. As he rose and placed one foot on the deck a violent squeal from Miracle mingled with a half-dozen shouts from men at poolside. Davis turned in time to see the calf ploughing water toward the boat. On impulse he grabbed a herring and held it at the water beside the boat. Miracle nimbly took that fish and a dozen more from Davis's hand before Davis threw one to centre pool. She regarded the sinking fish silently and then looked at Davis, but she made no move to retrieve it. He showed her another fish before heaving it into the water,

182

twenty feet away. Again she looked at Davis, and it was only a moment before she dipped her head into a dive that was marked faintly by a ripple.

The thirty-second dive seemed like an eternity and Wright was about to call for divers when the calf surfaced. She stopped long enough to throw a herring into the back of her mouth before sounding again. When she surfaced again it was to lift her entire body out of the water beside Davis's dinghy. As she went past, Davis threw his fishing hat over her snout. A few seconds later she surfaced with the hat between her teeth and readily exchanged it for a herring.

On one corner of the deck that surrounded the pool the medical-rescue crew had crowded into a back-slapping, self-congratulating group, which simultaneously cried and laughed over the victory.

Yet for Bill Davis the moment lingered, held fast by a deluge of memories. He remembered Miracle the first time he had seen her – a nameless, orphaned baby waiting, and wanting, to die. And he felt the growing sanctity of their friendship, which had begun that first day in Menzies Bay almost seven months earlier. Davis watched now as Miracle dove for the herring he threw, waited while she was hidden from view in the depths, and then marvelled at her graceful strength as her sleek body shot skyward in a burst of spray. But, to Davis, this moment held more than a flood of memories. It was something more substantial than a victorious end to a series of adverse events. It was the fulfilment of a dream, a frantic, faithful hope, on his part, that Miracle would live – and live to be happy.

Wright and Hoey watched silently from their poolside perch behind Davis's dinghy. They were awed by this creature whose existence short months earlier should have been ended by the disease and starvation that had plagued it. But they realized the real miracle was that another creature, who should, by all rights have been feared above all, became the whale's only hope of survival.

Now Miracle had found her home, in every sense of the word, not in her lifetime to be without the friendship and love of the people who had become her family.

RETROSPECT –
A Bloody History

Had Miracle been born slightly more than a decade earlier, her story could have been tragically different. The reasons encompass greed, fright, lack of knowledge – in many cases the desire not to know – and involve the geography of Vancouver Island.

The island juts boldly into the southwestern shore of British Columbia and pokes more than fifty miles below the forty-ninth parallel, forcing the Canada-United States border to jog sharply in its path. Although the western shore is inhospitably rugged – the relics of more than 250 ships lie in watery graves along the jagged coast – it serves as a weather and sea break for the "inside" waters of the island's east coast. Protected from the direct ravages of the Pacific Ocean, the inside waters have long been a year-round haven to sports and commercial fishermen and a myriad of sea animals – including killer whales.

In fact, the waters off the southeastern island are paradise to the killer whales, says Dr. Michael Bigg, head of killer whale research at the Pacific Biological Station in Nanaimo. His team of researchers and biologists have identified more than 250 killer whales living in the island's southern inside waters – more than in any other place in the world. The reason for the large population in the region is the easy access to food, mostly salmon.

And it is the killer whale's ferocious appetite for the fish and mammals – as well as other whales – that harbour in the protected waters, that has given this creature the dubious honour of being named "killer." Despite the implications, there has never been one authenticated case of the whales developing an appetite for humans. On the other hand, it is man who has developed a sorcerer's taste for the whales. In British Columbia, killer whales have never been killed for their oil and meat as they have been in the nearby state of Washington, points further north along western North Pacific, and in the northeastern North Atlantic. It seems the whales off Canada's western province were killed for sport or because of unfounded fears. The word "killer" frightened people – even those who should have known better – and they wanted to get even.

Had Miracle lived and matured during 1963 or early 1964 she would have found the whales' paradise a bloody realm indeed. For many years a few commercial fishermen had considered themselves God's appointed exterminators of killer whales. They took their appointments seriously and did their jobs well, but they could never quite do away with all the whales. Possibly buoyed by events in 1958, along the shores of Iceland, the fishermen decided to go to the Canadian Federal Fisheries Department.

The Icelandic government, pestered by its fishermen, who claimed the killer whales were devouring all the commercial fish, had enlisted the help of the United States. The American solution was to send airforce bombers to the rescue. After several months the two countries simultaneously reported the troublesome killer whales along the Icelandic shores had been bombed out of existence. Strangely enough, Iceland's fish production has not increased much in twenty years.

The Canadian fishermen knew they would also have

to have reasons for wanting the whales exterminated – not that Federal Fisheries needed reasons; it was just something to pacify the public conscience. In 1964, the Fisheries Department purchased a surplus armed forces Browning machine-gun because the fishermen had said the whales were depleting commercial stocks along the British Columbia coast, and among other things, the whales were a hazard to boating.

With a strong lobby and wide press coverage the fishermen were also able to sell their reasoning to an unthinking public. The machine-gun was scheduled to be mounted on a post at Race Point, about halfway along Vancouver Island's east coast. The post had been for just such a purpose and had held a machine-gun during the Second World War to help protect the shores against enemy invasion. The new plan for the post was to set up the machine-gun in such a way as to be able to annihilate each whale that swam through the narrow channel off the point. Ironically, the site was only several hundred yards from where Miracle was found and rescued almost fifteen years later.

Just as the Federal Fisheries officers were beginning to perspire from the heat of a hot kitchen – there were still thinking men and women who opposed their plan – Vancouver Aquarium authorities started their own brew boiling. Their plan, also covered extensively by the press, was to harpoon a killer whale, skin it and hang its skeleton in their museum. No one flinched and the public eagerly read accounts of the whalers' progress. The hunt extended almost half a year before a whale was harpooned. But the whale was only injured and it lived for three months in a pen in the Fraser River. It was believed to be a female, and was named Moby Doll, but intensive research revealed it to be a male.

Today its skeleton hangs in the aquarium museum.

Later, a killer whale was caught accidentally in a fisherman's net off the British Columbia fishing port of Namu. Given the name of the port, the whale was sold to an oceanarium in the nearby United States city of Seattle. By the end of the 1960s, whales were caught only for display. By 1970, the killing of whales had been outlawed and further legislation had reduced the number of killer whales to be caught to "replacement animals" – whales to replace ones that died in oceanariums. It was part of legislation introduced by the Canadian Fisheries Department for the protection of all marine mammals. But the laws were not yet enacted before the Fisheries Department – again at the urging of commercial fishermen – had a final bloody bout of slaughtering Stellar sea lions at the north end of Vancouver Island.

When Miracle was born paradise had been legally regained for the whales. Although the sanction of legal protection did not prevent Miracle from being critically wounded, the change in public attitudes allowed the orphan to be rescued. In a previous era the wounded calf would have been finished off in a round of spiteful target practice.

*   *   *

In preparing for the writing of this book I have learned that some people's attitudes have not changed much despite the legislation for the protection of whales. Word about the book began to precede me to various inter-views with fishermen and coastal sailors from whom I hoped to gain background historical knowledge of killer whales. These men and women were, for the most part, sympathetic to Miracle, and concerned about the plight of whales in general, but on too many occasions stories were related about how they continued to harm and harass whales.

The gruesome tales – some of them may have been no more than fictional hot air – detailed how men in high-speed power boats chased the whales to plunge boat hooks into the animals' backs, and how whales were used for target practice with rifles; how fins and tail flukes of baby whales were cut off before leaving the whale alone to die painfully and slowly. Each time a story of torture was recounted the teller would say, without prodding, that the torment inflicted had been a matter of sport – that in no way had the whales initiated the attacks.

On that hot August day when he first encountered Miracle, Davis was very much aware of the negative, sometimes destructive, ideas that some people had about killer whales, but he didn't know whether that was the norm or the exception of public opinion. There was no way he could know, until after the fact, how many people would morally and otherwise support his care of the dying baby whale or how many would oppose him. He was painfully aware all along that his efforts to save Miracle could cost him long-standing friendships and possibly force him and his family into being outcasts within the small town society. He could have turned away from the calf, easily rationalizing that she was beyond help. He also could have placed himself on a pedestal, daring anyone to oppose his cause. He did neither. His only concern was to save the baby's life and he went about the awesome task as quietly as he could, and in doing so, he displayed a rare brand of courage and conviction.

More than a year after the rescue Davis has become a quiet hero – a situation he accepts but one in which he finds little substance. He had set out simply to save a dying whale with no thought of personal glories. On November 14, 1977, Davis was presented with the British Columbia Society for Prevention of Cruelty to Animals (SPCA) award of merit – a special humanitarian award.

Another merit award was handed out by the SPCA on November 22, 1977 – this time it went to Sealand. It was presented for "outstanding and unselfish service in the care of Miracle, the baby killer whale," and was the first time the award had ever been given to other than an individual.

The much publicized award he received has contributed to Davis's status as a hero, but he, along with the medical-rescue team of Sealand, is more than aware of what tragedy there might have been had the baby whale been born when unfounded fears ruled the destiny of these ocean monarchs.

Paul Jeune
Malahat, July 1978